Enjoy Your Rights & Privileges

Live life within God's means...

Now!

Donna Crow

Enjoy Your Rights
& Privileges Now!

Live Within GOD'S Means . . .

By Donna Crow

Enjoy Your Rights & Privileges Now: Live Within God's Means

© 2013 by Donna Crow All rights reserved.
Protected by the Copyright laws of The United States of America.

No part of this book may be reproduced in any written, electronic, recording, or photocopying without written permission of the publisher or author. The exception would be in the case of brief quotations embodied in the critical articles or reviews and pages where permission is specifically granted by the publisher or author.

Although every precaution has been taken to verify the accuracy of the information contained herein, the author and publisher assume no responsibility for any errors or omissions. No liability is assumed for damages that may result from the use of information contained within.

Books may be purchased by contacting the publisher and author at:
http://www.donnacrow.com

All Scripture (Unless otherwise noted): New American Standard Bible (NASB)

Copyright © 1960, 1962, 1963, 1968, 1971, 1972, 1973, 1975, 1977, 1995

by The Lockman Foundation

Cover Design: Donna Crow
Interior Design: Donna Crow
Publisher: Donna Crow
Editor: Leslie Holzman, Katherine Register
Creative Consultant: The Holy Spirit

ISBN: 9780615917696
1. Christian, 2. Jesus, 3. Blessed, 4. Empowered,
First Edition
Printed in USA

Dedicated to all who seek freedom
through the knowledge of the Truth.

Acknowledgements

Many thanks go to:

    Leslie Holzmann,
    Jim Holzmann,
    Katherine Register,
    and Andrea Webster,

for their encouragement and their excellent help with editing.

Thanks also to Carol Shelton, for all your positivity and support.

Thank you Holy Spirit, for asking me to do this, and enabling me to do this.

Dear Reader

I live a very supernatural lifestyle.

- I take authority over bad weather and it changes to good.
- I command symptoms of illness to leave and they do.
- I ask for wisdom and receive it.
- I ask for direction and receive it.
- I receive warnings from Heaven, along with wisdom to intervene, resulting in different and better outcomes.
- I enjoy foreknowledge regarding friends, family, myself, and even the nation.
- I draw near to God and He draws near to me. I actually feel His love and His presence.
- I enjoy clear communication with Christ.
- I enjoy supernatural favor and grace.
- Etc.

Basically, I tap into the Kingdom of God and make use of the resources of Heaven on a daily basis.

Why? Because I believe the Word of God, which says,

> . . . all the promises of God are yes in Christ . . .
> Corinthians 1:20

That is a radical, yet true, statement, which I totally failed to see or comprehend for many, many years (though I read the Bible daily). It was far too large for me to believe, so it was simply invisible to me. Over time, under the guidance of the Holy Spirit, my concept of my inheritance in Christ slowly expanded until I could actually see this statement and begin to believe it.

One year, during the Christmas season, the Lord made it clear to me that He wanted me to fast. Fasting was not something I enjoyed, however, when the Lord asked me to fast, I was instantly delighted to comply. While I fasted, He revealed to me He wanted me to write down the fundamental rights and privileges of the Born-again believer. Starting with Genesis, I immediately began to scour the Bible looking for His promises. As I found them, I would write them down. It took me about a month to complete the list you have in your hands.

Since then, life has been quite an adventure. In my experience, enjoying the splendor of God's Kingdom (the Kingdom that I was transferred to when I was Born-again) has required a forcefulness with which I was not naturally born. In fact, back in the seventies I had one person tell me that I was the mellowest person they had ever met. If I were to describe myself during those younger years, I would say: *cheerful (sometimes to the point of hilarious), playful, creative, quiet and optimistic,* all positive qualities, but not qualities that naturally suit you for the rigors of Kingdom life. Over the years, however, life's challenges inspired me to experiment with the forcefulness required to apprehend Kingdom promises.

Led by the Holy Spirit, I have come to understand that enjoying my rights and privileges in Christ requires a focused intensity (enabled by the Holy Spirit) of will and purpose in believing His promises belong to me, and believing that I receive His promises. And sometimes it requires forcefully exercising authority over the enemy.

Like a person trained to fearlessly leap from one rooftop to another, I have learned to ignore my natural fears in order to make the leap from my emotional comfort zone to the reality of the unseen Kingdom of God, where His promises are my unearned inheritance in Christ.

> At times, forceful surrender has been needed.
> At other times forceful declaration,
> or forceful exercise of authority,
> or focused worship,

and none of these options have arisen in me naturally. I have had to press in to hear the voice of the Spirit of God, and resist my natural personality, in order to know the path, access God's Kingdom, and enjoy His promises. I believe the Word of God is true, and all His promises do belong to us in Christ, but they don't fall on us like ripe cherries off a tree. We must stir ourselves up to apprehend what is rightfully ours in Christ.

Foundational to all of this is the basic need to know what His promises are. It has been my experience that most people, myself included, don't even see many of God's promises when reading the Bible. Again, this is because those promises are so grand that their natural mind can't recognize them as actual reality available for and intended for them. This is a fundamental problem. If a promise is invisible to you, you are not likely to experience and enjoy that promise. *Enjoy Your Rights &*

Privileges Now is my effort, inspired by God, to bring His promises out of the shadows into the bright light of day where they can clearly be seen by any and all.

Why another promise book? I mean, hasn't this already been done? Well, yes and no. I have seen some lovely little promise books, however, many of the most remarkable promises are not included in these publications. I presume this is for the very reason I spoke of above. They were so grand they became invisible, and, therefore, were not included.

Within these pages you will find remarkable and profound promises of God listed for you. As I stated earlier, I live a very supernatural lifestyle, and so can you. God designed us for this, and is calling all of us to a lifestyle rife with His Presence, His Power, and His Promises fulfilled.

I encourage you to ask Him to help you to *Enjoy Your Rights & Privileges Now*. For more in-depth teaching on the subject of our inheritance in Christ, and how to live from God's means, please see our companion volumes listed at the back of this book.

Sincerely,
Donna Crow
http://www.donnacrow.com

> Joshua 1:8-9 NASB
>
> This book of the law shall not depart from your mouth, but you shall meditate on it day and night, so that you may be careful to do according to all that is written in it; for then you will make your way prosperous, and then you will have success.
>
> Have I not commanded you? Be strong and courageous! Do not tremble or be dismayed, for the Lord your God is with you wherever you go."

Instructions

I set this book up in sections for easy reference.

Sections 1-3 list all the rights and privileges for quick reference.

Sections 4-6 list the same rights and privileges, along with supporting verses.

You can quickly read through the list of promises in the first three sections for a quick overview. Personally, when I do this I find myself wanting to shout out loud with joy inspired by all that belongs to me in Christ.

Sections 4-6 contain the same list of rights and privileges along with the supporting verses. I find it wonderful to actually read the verses in the Bible that these statements are based on. Meditating in these verses helps your faith to grow leaps and bounds, and helps you to line up your own thinking and feeling with how God thinks and feels.

This is the bottom line: We will not live within God's means without knowing God's heart and mind, and then choosing to set our own heart and mind to agree with His.

Knowing the truth is foundational to freedom. In John 8:32, Jesus said, "... *you shall know the truth and the truth will make you free.*" God's will is His truth. When you know His will, you know the truth,.

His truth is foundational for being free and living within His means. Knowing truth, however, involves more than just taking in information. Information can be stored in the head, but not grasped by the heart. Because of that, my recommendation is that you go beyond merely reading this book. I recommend that you meditate on the truth it contains. Become so saturated with this truth that it is more real to you than the lack you see in the natural realm.

Walk in the light that you have, and be obedient to His voice. Open your mouth and begin to thank Him that He is faithful to His revealed will, and you will begin to see His supernatural provision in your life. He guarantees it.

Table of Contents

Section One
A Believer in Christ is: — Short Version	1

Section Two
The Believer's Rights & Privileges — Short Version	3

Section Three
The Believer and the Holy Spirit — Short Version	9

Section Four
A Believer in Christ is: — Long Version	13

Section Five
The Believer's Rights & Privileges — Long Version	39

Section Six
The Believer and the Holy Spirit — Long Version	105

Section Seven
What Then Shall We Say To All Of This?	137

Final Exhortation	147

Section One – A Believer is: – Short Version

Section One

First, let's define what it means to be a true believer in Christ:

An Individual

Who has heard the testimony of Jesus Christ as presented in the Bible (Especially in the first four books of the New Testament, known as the Gospels: Matthew, Mark, Luke, John).

Who has believed in Jesus the Christ	18
Has repented (Turning from darkness to light)	20
Accepted Jesus as their Savior	21
And their LORD	22
Who has been baptized in water	23
Who has openly declared their faith	24
Who has received forgiveness for their sins	24
Has been made righteous	25
Has been redeemed from the curse of the Law	26
Has been set free from the law of sin and death	31
Has experienced spiritual rebirth	31
Has been born of God	32

Section One – A Believer is: – Short Version

Has become a New Creation in Christ Jesus	32
Is now one spirit with Christ	33
Has passed out of death into life	33
Has been made complete (Perfect)	33
Is Holy and blameless and beyond reproach	34
Has received a Spirit of power, love and a sound mind	34
Has received a new heart	34
Has been made a child of God by adoption	34
Has become a fellow heir with Jesus Christ	35
Who is following Jesus as His disciple	36

Section Two

Having met the previously listed requirements, and thereby being esteemed, and in fact, a true Christian, you have the right and/or privilege to:

Seek God and find Him	39
Have God revealed to you	39
Have fellowship with God	39
Have confidence before God	40
Be refreshed by the Presence of God	40
Continually enjoy the tangible love of Jesus	41
Continually enjoy the tangible love of the Father	41
Hear the voice of God and follow Him	41
Have God speak through you	43
Live and abide in God's love	43
Experience God's never failing Mercy (NASB says, lovingkindness.)	45
Ask for and receive forgiveness	46
Be led by God daily	46

Section Two – The Believer's Rights & Privileges – Short Version

Ask in prayer and receive from God	48
Be protected by the power of God	50
Enjoy God's favor	50
Be molded into the image of Jesus Christ; to share inwardly His likeness.	51
Experience and express the fruit of the Spirit	51
Have honor and dignity restored	52
Be free from sin's dominion	53
Be transformed by the entire renewal of your mind	55
Be given strength in both body and soul	55
Experience good physical health through the power of God	57
Be prayed for by others in order to be healed	59
Pray with others in order for them to be healed	59
Pray for others while absent from them in order for them to be healed	60
Be free from all pain, disease, weakness, and infirmity.	61
Be immune to poisoning; as in: oral ingestion, bites and stings	63

Section Two – The Believer's Rights & Privileges – Short Version

Be able to bear children – Be Fertile	63
Raise the dead	64
Be free from demons (Unclean and evil spirits5	65
Have authority over unclean spirits in others	67
Perform signs, wonders, miracles and healing, in the name of Jesus Christ	68
Have your daily physical needs met	69
Even if it requires a miracle	70
Have life, and that more abundantly	73
Be free from poverty	74
Have your silver and gold increase	75
Have all that you possess multiplied	75
Be made rich	75
Gain enduring wealth	77
Have fortunes restored	79
Abound in prosperity	80
Be free of all lack	83
Have God bless everything you put your hand to	83
Be blessed with Abraham the believer	83

Section Two – The Believer's Rights & Privileges – Short Version

Enjoy all the blessings of God	85
Become a blessing, and bless others	87
Be supernaturally blessed; in the city or in the country	88
Have success in all your endeavors	88
Be given the desires of your heart by the Father	89
Inherit land	90
Possess a home filled with all precious and pleasant riches	91
Enjoy protection for your home	91
Have necessary rain in its season Freedom from drought	92
Have productive crops	93
Have abundance, even in days of famine	93
Have fruit trees produce a good yield	94
Take authority over weather and elements	94
Have harmful beasts eliminated from your land	95
Be protected from wild beasts	95
Have protection for your own animals	96

Section Two – The Believer's Rights & Privileges – Short Version

Have safety from and victory over enemies	96
Be protected from all evil	97
Be rescued	97
Be protected in war	97
Be protected by Angels	97
Be protected from the words of others	99
Be preserved, saved, delivered from trouble	99
Be delivered from the affliction of those who are stronger than you	100
Be free of fear	100
Not fear violence when it comes	101
Have peaceful sleep	102
Enjoy a long, satisfied, prosperous life	102
Have faith, which is the substance of things hoped for, the evidence of things not seen	104

Section Two – The Believer's Rights & Privileges – Short Version

Section Three - The Believer & The Holy Spirit – Short Version

Section Three

Having received the gift of the Holy Spirit in your heart (spirit) at the new birth, as a down payment and pledge of God's intent to fulfill all His promises, you have the right and or/privilege to:

Be baptized in the Holy Spirit Other terms include: To be "filled" with the Holy Spirit, or have the Holy Spirit "come upon" you.	106
Ask for and receive the Holy Spirit (As Baptizer)	108
Be taught by the Holy Spirit	108
Be guided into all the truth by the Holy Spirit	108
Know the truth	109
Be free	110
Walk in supernatural wisdom: to have the mind of Christ	111
Know the things freely given to you by God	113
Be informed about and prepared for the future. Personally and worldwide	113
Live a life of power with Jesus Christ	115
Exercise authority over all the powers of darkness and evil	115

Section Three - The Believer & The Holy Spirit – Short Version

Experience sanctification
Soul purification and restoration   116

Be comforted by God the Father   117

And the Holy Spirit   118

Be enabled to pray by the Holy Spirit   118

Pray in foreign human and Heavenly languages   119

Pray for and receive interpretation of these languages   121

Be rested, refreshed, edified and built-up   121

Receive revelation knowledge   122

Be made adequate as a servant of God's Covenant   123

Experience the manifestation of the Holy Spirit   124

To operate in a God ordained office   125

Be raised from the dead (Resurrected)   126

Be found listed in the Book of Life   127

Be free from judgment and condemnation   129

Escape the second death
Punishment of those who reject the Christ   129

Escape the lake of fire punishment   130

Be invited to, and to take part in, the Marriage Supper of the Lamb   131

Section Three - The Believer & The Holy Spirit – Short Version

Receive water from Jesus from the Fountain of
the Water of Life, without cost   131

Be allowed to eat of the Tree of Life,
in the midst of the Paradise of God   132

Receive an immortal, incorruptible body   132

Receive the Crown of Life   133

Live forever with Jesus Christ   133

Not hunger anymore, neither to thirst
anymore, neither to be smitten by the
sun, nor the scorching heat   134

Have every tear wiped away   135

Be free from anguish, grief, and pain   135

Be free from anything that is accursed
Detestable, foul, offensive, impure, hateful, horrible   136

Sit beside Jesus the Christ on His Throne   136

Section Three - The Believer & The Holy Spirit – Short Version

Section Four

A Believer in Christ is:

An individual who has heard the testimony of Jesus Christ as presented in the Bible (Especially in the first four books of the New Testament, known as the Gospels: Matthew, Mark, Luke, John)

John 3:3-21

3 Jesus answered and said to him, "Truly, truly, I say to you, unless one is born again he cannot see the kingdom of God."
4 Nicodemus said to Him, "How can a man be born when he is old? He cannot enter a second time into his mother's womb and be born, can he?"
5 Jesus answered, "Truly, truly, I say to you, unless one is born of water and the Spirit he cannot enter into the kingdom of God.
6 That which is born of the flesh is flesh, and that which is born of the Spirit is spirit.
7 Do not be amazed that I said to you, 'You must be born again.'
8 The wind blows where it wishes and you hear the sound of it, but do not know where it comes from and where it is going; so is everyone who is born of the Spirit."
9 Nicodemus said to Him, "How can these things be?"
10 Jesus answered and said to him, "Are you the teacher of Israel and do not understand these things?
11 Truly, truly, I say to you, we speak of what we know and testify of what we have seen, and you do not accept our testimony.
12 If I told you earthly things and you do not believe, how will you believe if I tell you heavenly things?

Section Four – A Believer in Christ is:

13 No one has ascended into heaven, but He who descended from heaven: the Son of Man.
14 As Moses lifted up the serpent in the wilderness, even so must the Son of Man be lifted up;
15 so that whoever believes will in Him have eternal life.
16 "For God so loved the world, that He gave His only begotten Son, that whoever believes in Him shall not perish, but have eternal life.
17 For God did not send the Son into the world to judge the world, but that the world might be saved through Him.
18 He who believes in Him is not judged; he who does not believe has been judged already, because he has not believed in the name of the only begotten Son of God.
19 This is the judgment, that the Light has come into the world, and men loved the darkness rather than the Light, for their deeds were evil.
20 For everyone who does evil hates the Light, and does not come to the Light for fear that his deeds will be exposed.
21 But he who practices the truth comes to the Light, so that his deeds may be manifested as having been wrought in God."

1 Peter 1:23

23 for you have been born again not of seed which is perishable but imperishable, that is, through the living and enduring word of God.

Luke 24:44-48

44 Now He said to them, "These are My words which I spoke to you while I was still with you, that all things which are written about Me in the Law of Moses and the Prophets and the Psalms must be fulfilled."
45 Then He opened their minds to understand the Scriptures,

Section Four – A Believer in Christ is:

46 and He said to them, "Thus it is written, that the Christ would suffer and rise again from the dead the third day,
47 and that repentance for forgiveness of sins would be proclaimed in His name to all the nations, beginning from Jerusalem.
48 You are witnesses of these things.

John 15:26-27

26 "When the Helper comes, whom I will send to you from the Father, that is the Spirit of truth who proceeds from the Father, He will testify about Me,
27 and you will testify also, because you have been with Me from the beginning.

John 20:30-31

30 Therefore many other signs Jesus also performed in the presence of the disciples, which are not written in this book;
31 but these have been written so that you may believe that Jesus is the Christ, the Son of God; and that believing you may have life in His name.

John 21:24-25

24 This is the disciple who is testifying to these things and wrote these things, and we know that his testimony is true.

25 And there are also many other things which Jesus did, which if they were written in detail, I suppose that even the world itself would not contain the books that would be written.

John 1:1-7

1 In the beginning was the Word, and the Word was with God, and the Word was God.
2 He was in the beginning with God.

Section Four – A Believer in Christ is:

3 All things came into being through Him, and apart from Him nothing came into being that has come into being.
4 In Him was life, and the life was the Light of men.
5 The Light shines in the darkness, and the darkness did not comprehend it.
6 There came a man sent from God, whose name was John.
7 He came as a witness, to testify about the Light, so that all might believe through him.

Acts 4:19-20

19 But Peter and John answered and said to them, "Whether it is right in the sight of God to give heed to you rather than to God, you be the judge;
20 for we cannot stop speaking about what we have seen and heard."

Isaiah 53:5-12

5 But He was pierced through for our transgressions, He was crushed for our iniquities; The chastening for our well-being fell upon Him, And by His scourging we are healed.
6 All of us like sheep have gone astray, Each of us has turned to his own way; But the LORD has caused the iniquity of us all To fall on Him.
7 He was oppressed and He was afflicted, Yet He did not open His mouth; Like a lamb that is led to slaughter, And like a sheep that is silent before its shearers, So He did not open His mouth.
8 By oppression and judgment He was taken away; And as for His generation, who considered That He was cut off out of the land of the living for the transgression of my people, to whom the stroke was due?
9 His grave was assigned with wicked men, Yet He was with a rich man in His death, Because He had done no violence, Nor was there any deceit in His mouth.
10 But the LORD was pleased to crush Him, putting Him to grief; If He would render Himself as a guilt

Section Four – A Believer in Christ is:

offering, He will see His offspring, He will prolong His days, And the good pleasure of the LORD will prosper in His hand.
11 As a result of the anguish of His soul, He will see it and be satisfied; By His knowledge the Righteous One, My Servant, will justify the many, As He will bear their iniquities.
12 Therefore, I will allot Him a portion with the great, And He will divide the booty with the strong; Because He poured out Himself to death, And was numbered with the transgressors; Yet He Himself bore the sin of many, And interceded for the transgressors.

1 Corinthians 15:1-11

1 Now I make known to you, brethren, the gospel which I preached to you, which also you received, in which also you stand,
2 by which also you are saved, if you hold fast the word, which I preached to you, unless you believed in vain.
3 For I delivered to you as of first importance what I also received, that Christ died for our sins according to the Scriptures,
4 and that He was buried, and that He was raised on the third day according to the Scriptures,
5 and that He appeared to Cephas, then to the twelve.
6 After that He appeared to more than five hundred brethren at one time, most of whom remain until now, but some have fallen asleep;
7 then He appeared to James, then to all the apostles;
8 and last of all, as to one untimely born, He appeared to me also.
9 For I am the least of the apostles, and not fit to be called an apostle, because I persecuted the church of God.
10 But by the grace of God I am what I am, and His grace toward me did not prove vain; but I labored even more than all of them, yet not I, but the grace of God with me.

Section Four – A Believer in Christ is:

11 Whether then it was I or they, so we preach and so you believed.

John 5:34

34 But the testimony which I receive is not from man, but I say these things so that you may be saved.

WHO HAS BELIEVED IN JESUS THE CHRIST

John 3:16-18

16 "For God so loved the world, that He gave His only begotten Son, that whoever believes in Him shall not perish, but have eternal life.
17 For God did not send the Son into the world to judge the world, but that the world might be saved through Him.
18 He who believes in Him is not judged; he who does not believe has been judged already, because he has not believed in the name of the only begotten Son of God.

John 20:29-31

29 Jesus said to him, "Because you have seen Me, have you believed? Blessed are they who did not see, and yet believed."
30 Therefore many other signs Jesus also performed in the presence of the disciples, which are not written in this book;
31 but these have been written so that you may believe that Jesus is the Christ, the Son of God; and that believing you may have life in His name.

Acts 16:30-33

30 and after he brought them out, he said, "Sirs, what must I do to be saved?"

Section Four – A Believer in Christ is:

31 They said, "Believe in the LORD Jesus, and you will be saved, you and your household."
32 And they spoke the word of the LORD to him together with all who were in his house.
33 And he took them that very hour of the night and washed their wounds, and immediately he was baptized, he and all his household.

Acts 13:38-39

38 Therefore let it be known to you, brethren, that through Him forgiveness of sins is proclaimed to you,
39 and through Him everyone who believes is freed from all things, from which you could not be freed through the Law of Moses.

Romans 3:21-23

21 But now apart from the Law the righteousness of God has been manifested, being witnessed by the Law and the Prophets,
22 even the righteousness of God through faith in Jesus Christ for all those who believe; for there is no distinction;
23 for all have sinned and fall short of the glory of God,

Romans 10:9

9 that if you confess with your mouth Jesus as LORD, and believe in your heart that God raised Him from the dead, you will be saved;

Galatians 2:16

16 nevertheless knowing that a man is not justified by the works of the Law but through faith in Christ Jesus, even we have believed in Christ Jesus, so that we may be justified by faith in Christ and not by the works of the Law; since by the works of the Law no flesh will be justified.

Section Four – A Believer in Christ is:

Galatians 3:22

22 But the Scripture has shut up everyone under sin, so that the promise by faith in Jesus Christ might be given to those who believe.

James 2:19-20

19 You believe that God is one. You do well; the demons also believe, and shudder.
20 But are you willing to recognize, you foolish fellow, that faith without works is useless?

1 John 3:23

23 This is His commandment, that we believe in the name of His Son Jesus Christ, and love one another, just as He commanded us.

HAS REPENTED, CHOOSING TO TURN FROM DARKNESS TO LIGHT

Acts 2:38

38 Peter said to them, "Repent, and each of you be baptized in the name of Jesus Christ for the forgiveness of your sins; and you will receive the gift of the Holy Spirit."

Acts 17:30

30 Therefore having overlooked the times of ignorance, God is now declaring to men that all people everywhere should repent,

Matthew 3:2

2 "Repent, for the kingdom of heaven is at hand."

Matthew 4:17

Section Four – A Believer in Christ is:

17 From that time Jesus began to preach and say, "Repent, for the kingdom of heaven is at hand."

Matthew 18:3

3 and said, "Truly I say to you, unless you are converted and become like children, you will not enter the kingdom of heaven.

Mark 6:12

12 They went out and preached that men should repent.

Luke 15:7,10

7 I tell you that in the same way, there will be more joy in heaven over one sinner who repents than over ninety-nine righteous persons who need no repentance.

Acts 3:19

19 Therefore repent and return, so that your sins may be wiped away, in order that times of refreshing may come from the presence of the LORD;

ACCEPTING JESUS AS THEIR SAVIOR

Acts 4:12

12 And there is salvation in no one else; for there is no other name under heaven that has been given among men by which we must be saved."

Luke 2:11

11 for today in the city of David there has been born for you a Savior, who is Christ the Lord.

Section Four – A Believer in Christ is:

1 John 4:14

14 We have seen and testify that the Father has sent the Son to be the Savior of the world.

Matthew 10:22

22 You will be hated by all because of My name, but it is the one who has endured to the end who will be saved.

John 4:42

42 and they were saying to the woman, "It is no longer because of what you said that we believe, for we have heard for ourselves and know that this One is indeed the Savior of the world."

Titus 1:4

4 To Titus, my true child in a common faith: Grace and peace from God the Father and Christ Jesus our Savior.

Titus 2:13

13 looking for the blessed hope and the appearing of the glory of our great God and Savior, Christ Jesus,

2 Peter 1:11

11 for in this way the entrance into the eternal kingdom of our LORD and Savior Jesus Christ will be abundantly supplied to you.

AND THEIR LORD

Acts 2:36

Section Four – A Believer in Christ is:

36 Therefore let all the house of Israel know for certain that God has made Him both LORD and Christ—this Jesus whom you crucified."

Luke 2:11

11 for today in the city of David there has been born for you a Savior, who is Christ the LORD.

John 20:28

28 And Thomas answered and said to Him, "My Lord and my God!"

Romans 10:9

9 that if you confess with your mouth Jesus as Lord, and believe in your heart that God raised Him from the dead, you will be saved;

Philippians 2:11

11 and that every tongue will confess that Jesus Christ is Lord, to the glory of God the Father.

WHO HAS BEEN BAPTIZED IN WATER

Mark 16:16

16 He who has believed and has been baptized shall be saved; but he who has disbelieved shall be condemned.

Acts 2:38

38 Peter said to them, "Repent, and each of you be baptized in the name of Jesus Christ for the forgiveness of your sins; and you will receive the gift of the Holy Spirit.

Section Four – A Believer in Christ is:

WHO HAS OPENLY DECLARED THEIR FAITH

Matthew 10:32-38

32 "Therefore everyone who confesses Me before men, I will also confess him before My Father who is in heaven.
33 But whoever denies Me before men, I will also deny him before My Father who is in heaven.
34 "Do not think that I came to bring peace on the earth; I
did not come to bring peace, but a sword.
35 For I came to set a man against his father, and a daughter against her mother, and a daughter-in-law against her mother-in-law;
36 and a man's enemies will be the members of his household.
37 "He who loves father or mother more than Me is not worthy of Me; and he who loves son or daughter more than Me is not worthy of Me.
38 And he who does not take his cross and follow after Me is not worthy of Me.

WHO HAS RECEIVED FORGIVENESS FOR THEIR SINS

Luke 24:46-47

46 and He said to them, "Thus it is written, that the Christ would suffer and rise again from the dead the third day,
47 and that repentance for forgiveness of sins would be proclaimed in His name to all the nations, beginning from Jerusalem.

Acts 10:43

Section Four – A Believer in Christ is:

43 Of Him all the prophets bear witness that through His name everyone who believes in Him receives forgiveness of sins."

Matthew 26:28

28 for this is My blood of the covenant, which is poured out for many for forgiveness of sins.

Acts 13:38

38 Therefore let it be known to you, brethren, that through Him forgiveness of sins is proclaimed to you,

Acts 26:18

18 to open their eyes so that they may turn from darkness to light and from the dominion of Satan to God, that they may receive forgiveness of sins and an inheritance among those who have been sanctified by faith in Me.'

Ephesians 1:7

7 In Him we have redemption through His blood, the forgiveness of our trespasses, according to the riches of His grace

Colossians 1:14

14 in whom we have redemption, the forgiveness of sins.

HAS BEEN MADE RIGHTEOUS

2 Corinthians 5:21

21 He made Him who knew no sin to be sin on our behalf, so that we might become the righteousness of God in Him.

Section Four – A Believer in Christ is:

Romans 5:19

19 For as through the one man's disobedience the many were made sinners, even so through the obedience of the One the many will be made righteous.

Romans 10:3 & 10

3 For not knowing about God's righteousness and seeking to establish their own, they did not subject themselves to the righteousness of God.

10 for with the heart a person believes, resulting in righteousness, and with the mouth he confesses, resulting in salvation.

1 Corinthians 1:30

30 But by His doing you are in Christ Jesus, who became to us wisdom from God, and righteousness and sanctification, and redemption,

HAS BEEN REDEEMED FROM THE CURSE OF THE LAW

Galatians 3:13

13 Christ redeemed us from the curse of the Law, having become a curse for us—for it is written, "Cursed is everyone who hangs on a tree"

Read Genesis 1 through Deuteronomy 34
Which we have not included here.

Deuteronomy 28:15-68

15 "But it shall come about, if you do not obey the LORD your God, to observe to do all His

Section Four – A Believer in Christ is:

commandments and His statutes with which I charge you today, that all these curses will come upon you and overtake you:

16 "Cursed shall you be in the city, and cursed shall you be in the country.

17 "Cursed shall be your basket and your kneading bowl.

18 "Cursed shall be the offspring of your body and the produce of your ground, the increase of your herd and the young of your flock.

19 "Cursed shall you be when you come in, and cursed shall you be when you go out.

20 "The LORD will send upon you curses, confusion, and rebuke, in all you undertake to do, until you are destroyed and until you perish quickly, on account of the evil of your deeds, because you have forsaken Me.

21 The LORD will make the pestilence cling to you until He has consumed you from the land where you are entering to possess it.

22 The LORD will smite you with consumption and with fever and with inflammation and with fiery heat and with the sword and with blight and with mildew, and they will pursue you until you perish.

23 The heaven which is over your head shall be bronze, and the earth which is under you, iron.

24 The LORD will make the rain of your land powder and dust; from heaven it shall come down on you until you are destroyed.

25 "The LORD shall cause you to be defeated before your enemies; you will go out one way against them, but you will flee seven ways before them, and you will be an example of terror to all the kingdoms of the earth.

26 Your carcasses will be food to all birds of the sky and to the beasts of the earth, and there will be no one to frighten them away.

27 "The LORD will smite you with the boils of Egypt and with tumors and with the scab and with the itch, from which you cannot be healed.

28 The LORD will smite you with madness and with blindness and with bewilderment of heart;

Section Four – A Believer in Christ is:

29 and you will grope at noon, as the blind man gropes in darkness, and you will not prosper in your ways; but you shall only be oppressed and robbed continually, with none to save you.
30 You shall betroth a wife, but another man will violate her; you shall build a house, but you will not live in it; you shall plant a vineyard, but you will not use its fruit.
31 Your ox shall be slaughtered before your eyes, but you will not eat of it; your donkey shall be torn away from you, and will not be restored to you; your sheep shall be given to your enemies, and you will have none to save you.
32 Your sons and your daughters shall be given to another people, while your eyes look on and yearn for them continually; but there will be nothing you can do.
33 A people whom you do not know shall eat up the produce of your ground and all your labors, and you will never be anything but oppressed and crushed continually.
34 You shall be driven mad by the sight of what you see.
35 The LORD will strike you on the knees and legs with sore boils, from which you cannot be healed, from the sole of your foot to the crown of your head.
36 The LORD will bring you and your king, whom you set over you, to a nation which neither you nor your fathers have known, and there you shall serve other gods, wood and stone.
37 You shall become a horror, a proverb, and a taunt among all the people where the LORD drives you.
38 "You shall bring out much seed to the field but you will gather in little, for the locust will consume it.
39 You shall plant and cultivate vineyards, but you will neither drink of the wine nor gather the grapes, for the worm will devour them.
40 You shall have olive trees throughout your territory but you will not anoint yourself with the oil, for your olives will drop off.
41 You shall have sons and daughters but they will not be yours, for they will go into captivity.

Section Four – A Believer in Christ is:

42 The cricket shall possess all your trees and the produce of your ground.
43 The alien who is among you shall rise above you higher and higher, but you will go down lower and lower.
44 He shall lend to you, but you will not lend to him; he shall be the head, and you will be the tail.
45 "So all these curses shall come on you and pursue you and overtake you until you are destroyed, because you would not obey the LORD your God by keeping His commandments and His statutes which He commanded you.
46 They shall become a sign and a wonder on you and your descendants forever.
47 "Because you did not serve the LORD your God with joy and a glad heart, for the abundance of all things;
48 therefore you shall serve your enemies whom the LORD will send against you, in hunger, in thirst, in nakedness, and in the lack of all things; and He will put an iron yoke on your neck until He has destroyed you.
49 "The LORD will bring a nation against you from afar, from the end of the earth, as the eagle swoops down, a nation whose language you shall not understand,
50 a nation of fierce countenance
who will have no respect for the old, nor show favor to the young.
51 Moreover, it shall eat the offspring of your herd and the produce of your ground until you are destroyed, who also leaves you no grain, new wine, or oil, nor the increase of your herd or the young of your flock until they have caused you to perish.
52 It shall besiege you in all your towns until your high and fortified walls in which you trusted come down throughout your land, and it shall besiege you in all your towns throughout your land which the LORD your God has given you.
53 Then you shall eat the offspring of your own body, the flesh of your sons and of your daughters whom the LORD your God has given you, during the siege and the distress by which your enemy will oppress you.

Section Four – A Believer in Christ is:

54 The man who is refined and very delicate among you shall be hostile toward his brother and toward the wife he cherishes and toward the rest of his children who remain,
55 so that he will not give even one of them any of the flesh of his children which he will eat, since he has nothing else left, during the siege and the distress by which your enemy will oppress you in all your towns.
56 The refined and delicate woman among you, who would not venture to set the sole of her foot on the ground for delicateness and refinement, shall be hostile toward the husband she cherishes and toward her son and daughter,
57 and toward her afterbirth which issues from between her legs and toward her children whom she bears; for she will eat them secretly for lack of anything else, during the siege and the distress by which your enemy will oppress you in your towns.
58 "If you are not careful to observe all the words of this law which are written in this book, to fear this honored and awesome name, the LORD your God,
59 then the LORD will bring extraordinary plagues on you and your descendants, even severe and lasting plagues, and miserable and chronic sicknesses.
60 He will bring back on you all the diseases of Egypt of which you were afraid, and they will cling to you.
61 Also every sickness and every plague which, not written in the book of this law, the LORD will bring on you until you are destroyed. 62 Then you shall be left few in number, whereas you were as numerous as the stars of heaven, because you did not obey the LORD your God.
63 It shall come about that as the LORD delighted over you to prosper you, and multiply you, so the LORD will delight over you to make you perish and destroy you; and you will be torn from the land where you are entering to possess it.
64 Moreover, the LORD will scatter you among all peoples, from one end of the earth to the other end of the earth; and there you shall serve other gods, wood and stone, which you or your fathers have not known.

Section Four – A Believer in Christ is:

65 Among those nations you shall find no rest, and there will be no resting place for the sole of your foot; but there the LORD will give you a trembling heart, failing of eyes, and despair of soul.
66 So your life shall hang in doubt before you; and you will be in dread night and day, and shall have no assurance of your life.
67 In the morning you shall say, 'Would that it were evening!' And at evening you shall say, 'Would that it were morning!' because of the dread of your heart which you dread, and for the sight of your eyes which you will see.
68 The LORD will bring you back to Egypt in ships, by the way about which I spoke to you, 'You will never see it again!' And there you will offer yourselves for sale to your enemies as male and female slaves, but there will be no buyer."

HAS BEEN SET FREE FROM THE LAW OF SIN AND DEATH

Romans 8:2

2 For the law of the Spirit of life in Christ Jesus has set you free from the law of sin and of death.

HAS EXPERIENCED SPIRITUAL REBIRTH

John 3:3-8 and 36

3 Jesus answered and said to him, "Truly, truly, I say to you, unless one is born again he cannot see the kingdom of God."
4 Nicodemus said to Him, "How can a man be born when he is old? He cannot enter a second time into his mother's womb and be born, can he?"
5 Jesus answered, "Truly, truly, I say to you, unless one is born of water and the Spirit he cannot enter into the kingdom of God.

Section Four – A Believer in Christ is:

6 That which is born of the flesh is flesh, and that which is born of the Spirit is spirit.
7 Do not be amazed that I said to you, 'You must be born again.'
8 The wind blows where it wishes and you hear the sound of it, but do not know where it comes from and where it is going; so is everyone who is born of the Spirit.
36 He who believes in the Son has eternal life; but he who does not obey the Son will not see life, but the wrath of God abides on him."

John 5:24

24 "Truly, truly, I say to you, he who hears My word, and believes Him who sent Me, has eternal life, and does not come into judgment, but has passed out of death into life.

Romans 8:10

10 If Christ is in you, though the body is dead because of sin, yet the spirit is alive because of righteousness.

HAS BEEN BORN OF GOD

1 John 5:1

5 Whoever believes that Jesus is the Christ is born of God, and whoever loves the Father loves the child born of Him.

HAS BECOME A NEW CREATION IN CHRIST JESUS

2 Corinthians 5:17

Section Four – A Believer in Christ is:

17 Therefore if anyone is in Christ, he is a new creature; the old things passed away; behold, new things have come.

Galatians 6:14-15

14 But may it never be that I would boast, except in the cross of our Lord Jesus Christ, through which the world has been crucified to me, and I to the world.
15 For neither is circumcision anything, nor uncircumcision, but a new creation.

IS NOW ONE SPIRIT WITH CHRIST

1 Corinthians 6:17

17 But the one who joins himself to the Lord is one spirit with Him.

HAS PASSED OUT OF DEATH INTO LIFE

1 John 3:14

14 We know that we have passed out of death into life, because we love the brethren. He who does not love abides in death.

HAS BEEN MADE COMPLETE - PERFECT

Colossians 2:10

10 and in Him you have been made complete, and He is the head over all rule and authority;

Hebrews 12:23

Section Four – A Believer in Christ is:

23 to the general assembly and church of the firstborn who are enrolled in heaven, and to God, the Judge of all, and to the spirits of the righteous made perfect,

IS HOLY AND BLAMELESS AND BEYOND REPROACH

Colossians 1:22

22 yet He has now reconciled you in His fleshly body through death, in order to present you before Him holy and blameless and beyond reproach—

HAS RECEIVED A SPIRIT OF POWER, LOVE AND A SOUND MIND

2 Timothy 1:7 KJV

7 For God hath not given us the spirit of fear; but of power, and of love, and of a sound mind.

HAS RECEIVED A NEW HEART

Ezekiel 36:26

26 Moreover, I will give you a new heart and put a new spirit within you; and I will remove the heart of stone from your flesh and give you a heart of flesh.

HAS BEEN MADE A CHILD OF GOD BY ADOPTION

John 1:12

12 But as many as received Him, to them He gave the right to become children of God, even to those who believe in His name,

Section Four – A Believer in Christ is:

Mark 3:35

35 For whoever does the will of God, he is My brother and sister and mother."

Romans 8:15-17

15 For you have not received a spirit of slavery leading to fear again, but you have received a spirit of adoption as sons by which we cry out, "Abba! Father!"
16 The Spirit Himself testifies with our spirit that we are children of God,
17 and if children, heirs also, heirs of God and fellow heirs with Christ, if indeed we suffer with Him so that we may also be glorified with Him.

HAS BECOME A FELLOW HEIR WITH JESUS CHRIST

Romans 8:17

17 and if children, heirs also, heirs of God and fellow heirs with Christ, if indeed we suffer with Him so that we may also be glorified with Him.

Galatians 3:29

29 And if you belong to Christ, then you are Abraham's descendants, heirs according to promise.

Galatians 4:7

7 Therefore you are no longer a slave, but a son; and if a son, then an heir through God.

Ephesians 3:6

Section Four – A Believer in Christ is:

6 to be specific, that the Gentiles are fellow heirs and fellow members of the body, and fellow partakers of the promise in Christ Jesus through the gospel,

Titus 3:7

7 so that being justified by His grace we would be made heirs according to the hope of eternal life.

Revelation 21:7

7 He who overcomes will inherit these things, and I will be his God and he will be My son.

John 3:16

16 "For God so loved the world, that He gave His only begotten Son, that whoever believes in Him shall not perish, but have eternal life.

John 5:18

18 For this reason therefore the Jews were seeking all the more to kill Him, because He not only was breaking the Sabbath, but also was calling God His own Father, making Himself equal with God.

WHO IS FOLLOWING JESUS AS HIS DISCIPLE
STUDENT FOLLOWER

Matthew 28:19-20

19 Go therefore and make disciples of all the nations, baptizing them in the name of the Father and the Son and the Holy Spirit,
20 teaching them to observe all that I commanded you; and lo, I am with you always, even to the end of the age."

Section Four – A Believer in Christ is:

Luke 9:23

23 And He was saying to them all, "If anyone wishes to come after Me, he must deny himself, and take up his cross daily and follow Me.

Luke 14:26

26 "If anyone comes to Me, and does not hate his own father and mother and wife and children and brothers and sisters, yes, and even his own life, he cannot be My disciple.

John 8:30-32

30 As He spoke these things, many came to believe in Him.
31 So Jesus was saying to those Jews who had believed Him, "If you continue in My word, then you are truly disciples of Mine;
32 and you will know the truth, and the truth will make you free."

John 10:27

27 My sheep hear My voice, and I know them, and they follow Me;

Section Four – A Believer in Christ is:

Section Five

Having met the previously listed requirements, and thereby being esteemed, and in fact, a true Christian, you have the right and/or privilege to:

SEEK GOD AND FIND HIM

Deuteronomy 4:29

29 But from there you will seek the LORD your God, and you will find Him if you search for Him with all your heart and all your soul.

James 4:8

8 Draw near to God and He will draw near to you. Cleanse your hands, you sinners; and purify your hearts, you double-minded.

HAVE GOD REVEALED TO YOU

John 14:21

21 He who has My commandments and keeps them is the one who loves Me; and he who loves Me will be loved by My Father, and I will love him and will disclose Myself to him."

HAVE FELLOWSHIP WITH GOD

1 John 1:3

3 what we have seen and heard we proclaim to you also, so that you too may have fellowship with us; and

indeed our fellowship is with the Father, and with His Son Jesus Christ.

Matthew 28:20

20 teaching them to observe all that I commanded you; and lo, I am with you always, even to the end of the age."

John 15:14

14 You are My friends if you do what I command you.

James 4:8A

8 Draw near to God and He will draw near to you.

Revelation 3:20

20 Behold, I stand at the door and knock; if anyone hears My voice and opens the door, I will come in to him and will dine with him, and he with Me.

HAVE CONFIDENCE BEFORE GOD

Ephesians 3:12

12 in whom we have boldness and confident access through faith in Him.

I John 3:21

21 Beloved, if our heart does not condemn us, we have confidence before God;

BE REFRESHED
BY THE PRESENCE OF GOD

Acts 3:19

Section Five – The Believer's Rights & Privileges

19 Therefore repent and return, so that your sins may be wiped away, in order that times of refreshing may come from the presence of the LORD;

CONTINUALLY ENJOY THE TANGIBLE LOVE OF JESUS

John 15:10

10 If you keep My commandments, you will abide in My love; just as I have kept My Father's commandments and abide in His love.

CONTINUALLY ENJOY THE TANGIBLE LOVE OF THE FATHER

John 14:23

23 Jesus answered and said to him, "If anyone loves Me, he will keep My word; and My Father will love him, and We will come to him and make Our abode with him.

HEAR THE VOICE OF GOD AND FOLLOW HIM

Exodus 15:26

26 And He said, "If you will give earnest heed to the voice of the LORD your God, and do what is right in His sight, and give ear to His commandments, and keep all His statutes, I will put none of the diseases on you which I have put on the Egyptians; for I, the LORD, am your healer."

Exodus 19:5

Section Five – The Believer's Rights & Privileges

5 Now then, if you will indeed obey My voice and keep My covenant, then you shall be My own possession among all the peoples, for all the earth is Mine;

Deuteronomy 30:20

20 by loving the LORD your God, by obeying His voice, and by holding fast to Him; for this is your life and the length of your days, that you may live in the land which the LORD swore to your fathers, to Abraham, Isaac, and Jacob, to give them."

Genesis 9:8

8 Then God spoke to Noah and to his sons with him, saying,

Genesis 35:13

13 Then God went up from him in the place where He had spoken with him.

1Kings 8:15

15 He said, "Blessed be the LORD, the God of Israel, who spoke with His mouth to my father David and has fulfilled it with His hand, saying,

Job 42:7

7 It came about after the LORD had spoken these words to Job, that the LORD said to Eliphaz the Temanite, "My wrath is kindled against you and against your two friends, because you have not spoken of Me what is right as My servant Job has.

Job 33:14

14 "Indeed God speaks once, Or twice, yet no one notices it.

Isaiah 30:21

Section Five – The Believer's Rights & Privileges

21 Your ears will hear a word behind you, "This is the way, walk in it," whenever you turn to the right or to the left.

John 16:13

13 But when He, the Spirit of truth, comes, He will guide you into all the truth; for He will not speak on His own initiative, but whatever He hears, He will speak; and He will disclose to you what is to come.

HAVE GOD SPEAK THROUGH YOU

Matthew 10:20

20 For it is not you who speak, but it is the Spirit of your Father who speaks in you.

John 3:34

34 For He whom God has sent speaks the words of God; for He gives the Spirit without measure.

1 Peter 4:11

11 Whoever speaks, is to do so as one who is speaking the utterances of God; whoever serves is to do so as one who is serving by the strength which God supplies; so that in all things God may be glorified through Jesus Christ, to whom belongs the glory and dominion forever and ever. Amen.

LIVE AND ABIDE IN GOD'S LOVE

John 15:10

Section Five – The Believer's Rights & Privileges

10 If you keep My commandments, you will abide in My love; just as I have kept My Father's commandments and abide in His love.

Romans 8:38-39

38 For I am convinced that neither death, nor life, nor angels, nor principalities, nor things present, nor things to come, nor powers, 39 nor height, nor depth, nor any other created thing, will be able to separate us from the love of God, which is in Christ Jesus our LORD.

1 John 4:7-21

7 Beloved, let us love one another, for love is from God; and everyone who loves is born of God and knows God.
8 The one who does not love does not know God, for God is love.
9 By this the love of God was manifested in us, that God has sent His only begotten Son into the world so that we might live through Him.
10 In this is love, not that we loved God, but that He loved us and sent His Son to be the propitiation for our sins.
11 Beloved, if God so loved us, we also ought to love one another.
12 No one has seen God at any time; if we love one another, God abides in us, and His love is perfected in us.
13 By this we know that we abide in Him and He in us, because He has given us of His Spirit.
14 We have seen and testify that the Father has sent the Son to be the Savior of the world.
15 Whoever confesses that Jesus is the Son of God, God abides in him, and he in God.
16 We have come to know and have believed the love which God has for us. God is love, and the one who abides in love abides in God, and God abides in him.

Section Five – The Believer's Rights & Privileges

17 By this, love is perfected with us, so that we may have confidence in the day of judgment; because as He is, so also are we in this world.
18 There is no fear in love; but perfect love casts out fear, because fear involves punishment, and the one who fears is not perfected in love.
19 We love, because He first loved us.
20 If someone says, "I love God," and hates his brother, he is a liar; for the one who does not love his brother whom he has seen, cannot love God whom he has not seen.
21 And this commandment we have from Him, that the one who loves God should love his brother also.

Jude 21

21 keep yourselves in the love of God, waiting anxiously for the mercy of our LORD Jesus Christ to eternal life.

EXPERIENIENCE GOD'S NEVER FAILING MERCY
(NASB SAYS, LOVINGKIDNESS)

Luke 1:50

50 "And His mercy is upon generation after generation toward those who fear Him.

1Chronicles 16:34

34 Oh, give thanks to the LORD, for He is good! For His mercy endures forever. (NKJV)

Psalm 25:10

10 All the paths of the LORD are mercy and truth, to such as keep His covenant and His testimonies. (NKJV)

Psalm 32:10

Section Five – The Believer's Rights & Privileges

10 Many sorrows shall be to the wicked; But he who trusts in the LORD, mercy shall surround him. (NKJV)

ASK FOR AND RECEIVE FORGIVENESS

1 John 1:9

9 If we confess our sins, He is faithful and righteous to forgive us our sins and to cleanse us from all unrighteousness.

Mark 11:25-26

25 Whenever you stand praying, forgive, if you have anything against anyone, so that your Father who is in heaven will also forgive you your transgressions.
26 [But if you do not forgive, neither will your Father who is in heaven forgive your transgressions."]

1 John 2:1-2

1 My little children, I am writing these things to you so that you may not sin. And if anyone sins, we have an Advocate with the Father, Jesus Christ the righteous;
2 and He Himself is the propitiation for our sins; and not for ours only, but also for those of the whole world.

BE LED BY GOD DAILY

John 16:13

13 But when He, the Spirit of truth, comes, He will guide you into all the truth; for He will not speak on His own initiative, but whatever He hears, He will speak; and He will disclose to you what is to come.

Romans 8:14

Section Five – The Believer's Rights & Privileges

14 For all who are being led by the Spirit of God, these are sons of God.

John 12:26

26 If anyone serves Me, he must follow Me; and where I am, there My servant will be also; if anyone serves Me, the Father will honor him.

Psalm 25:12

12 Who is the man who fears the LORD? He will instruct him in the way he should choose.

Psalm 31:3

3 For You are my rock and my fortress; For Your name's sake You will lead me and guide me.

Isaiah 30:21

21 Your ears will hear a word behind you, "This is the way, walk in it," whenever you turn to the right or to the left.

Isaiah 48:17

17 Thus says the LORD, your Redeemer, the Holy One of Israel, "I am the LORD your God, who teaches you to profit, Who leads you in the way you should go.

Psalm 32:8

8 I will instruct you and teach you in the way which you should go; I will counsel you with My eye upon you.

Psalm 48:14

Section Five – The Believer's Rights & Privileges

14 For such is God, Our God forever and ever; He will guide us until death.

Psalm 73:24

24 With Your counsel You will guide me, And afterward receive me to glory.

ASK IN PRAYER AND RECEIVE FROM GOD

Matthew 7:7-11

7 "Ask, and it will be given to you; seek, and you will find; knock, and it will be opened to you.
8 For everyone who asks receives, and he who seeks finds, and to him who knocks it will be opened.
9 Or what man is there among you who, when his son asks for a loaf, will give him a stone?
10 Or if he asks for a fish, he will not give him a snake, will he?
11 If you then, being evil, know how to give good gifts to your children, how much more will your Father who is in heaven give what is good to those who ask Him!

Mark 11:22-24

22 And Jesus answered saying to them, "Have faith in God.
23 Truly I say to you, whoever says to this mountain, 'Be taken up and cast into the sea,' and does not doubt in his heart, but believes that what he says is going to happen, it will be granted him.
24 Therefore I say to you, all things for which you pray and ask, believe that you have received them, and they will be granted you.

AUTHOR'S NOTE: The word "ask," in verse 24 above is more properly translated as "require" or "call for". You can clearly

Section Five – The Believer's Rights & Privileges

see this is the correct meaning of the word by the fact that Jesus said, *whoever says*, followed by a declaration or command. Notice He is not instructing us to supplicate regarding mountains, but rather to command them with authority. There are places to supplicate, and there are places to command. Study the gospels and notice where supplication was made and when commands were given, and ask the Holy Spirit to give you revelation as to when to supplicate and when to command in your own life. Your success in the area of prayer will greatly increase if you do so.

Matthew 18:19

19 "Again I say to you, that if two of you agree on earth about anything that they may ask, it shall be done for them by My Father who is in heaven.

Matthew 21:22

22 And all things you ask in prayer, believing, you will receive."

John 14:13

13 Whatever you ask in My name, that will I do, so that the Father may be glorified in the Son.

John 15:7-8, 16

7 If you abide in Me, and My words abide in you, ask whatever you wish, and it will be done for you.
8 My Father is glorified by this, that you bear much fruit, and so prove to be My disciples.

16 You did not choose Me but I chose you, and appointed you that you would go and bear fruit, and that your fruit would remain, so that whatever you ask of the Father in My name He may give to you.

John 16:23-24

Section Five – The Believer's Rights & Privileges

23 In that day you will not question Me about anything. Truly, truly, I say to you, if you ask the Father for anything in My name, He will give it to you. 24 Until now you have asked for nothing in My name; ask and you will receive, so that your joy may be made full.

Job 22:28

28 "You will also decree a thing, and it will be established for you; And light will shine on your ways.

BE PROTECTED BY THE POWER OF GOD

1 Peter 1:5

5 who are protected by the power of God through faith for a salvation ready to be revealed in the last time.

ENJOY GOD'S FAVOR

Psalm 5:12

12 For it is You who blesses the righteous man, O LORD, You surround him with favor as with a shield.

Psalm 147:11

11 The LORD favors those who fear Him, Those who wait for His lovingkindness

Proverbs 3:4

4 So you will find favor and good repute in the sight of God and man.

Proverbs 8:35

35 "For he who finds me finds life and obtains favor from the LORD.

Proverbs 12:2a

2 A good man will obtain favor from the LORD

BE MOLDED INTO THE IMAGE OF JESUS CHRIST
AND SHARE, INWARDLY, HIS LIKENESS

Romans 8:29
Amplified Bible (AMP)

29 For those whom He foreknew [of whom He was aware and loved beforehand], He also destined from the beginning [foreordaining them] to be molded into the image of His Son [and share inwardly His likeness], that He might become the firstborn among many brethren.

Colossians 3:10

10 and have put on the new self who is being renewed to a true knowledge according to the image of the One who created him—

EXPERIENCE AND EXPRESS THE FRUIT OF THE SPIRIT

Galatians 5:22-23

22 But the fruit of the Spirit is love, joy, peace, patience, kindness, goodness, faithfulness,
23 gentleness, self-control; against such things there is no law.

John 15:1-5

1"I am the true vine, and My Father is the vinedresser.

Section Five – The Believer's Rights & Privileges

2 Every branch in Me that does not bear fruit, He takes away; and every branch that bears fruit, He prunes it so that it may bear more fruit.
3 You are already clean because of the word which I have spoken to you.
4 Abide in Me, and I in you. As the branch cannot bear fruit of itself unless it abides in the vine, so neither can you unless you abide in Me.
5 I am the vine, you are the branches; he who abides in Me and I in him, he bears much fruit, for apart from Me you can do nothing.

    Examples: Love
                          Joy
                          Peace
                          Patience
                          Kindness
                          Goodness
                          Gentleness
                          Faithfulness
                          Self-Control

HAVE HONOR AND DIGNITY RESTORED

Psalm 91:15

15 "He will call upon Me, and I will answer him; I will be with him in trouble; I will rescue him and honor him.

Proverbs 3:35

35 The wise will inherit honor, but fools display dishonor.

Proverbs 11:16

16 A gracious woman attains honor, and ruthless men attain riches.

Proverbs 13:18

Section Five – The Believer's Rights & Privileges

18 Poverty and shame will come to him who neglects discipline, But he who regards reproof will be honored.

Proverbs 21:21

21 He who pursues righteousness and loyalty finds life, righteousness and honor.

Deuteronomy 26:19

19 and that He will set you high above all nations which He has made, for praise, fame, and honor; and that you shall be a consecrated people to the LORD your God, as He has spoken."

BE FREE FROM SIN'S DOMINION

Romans 6:14

14 For sin shall not be master over you, for you are not under law but under grace.

Galatians 5:19-21

19 Now the deeds of the flesh are evident, which are: immorality, impurity, sensuality,
20 idolatry, sorcery, enmities, strife, jealousy, outbursts of anger, disputes, dissensions, factions,
21 envying, drunkenness, carousing, and things like these, of which I forewarn you, just as I have forewarned you, that those who practice such things will not inherit the kingdom of God.

1 Corinthians 10:13

13 No temptation has overtaken you but such as is common to man; and God is faithful, who will not allow you to be tempted beyond what you are able, but with

Section Five – The Believer's Rights & Privileges

the temptation will provide the way of escape also, so that you will be able to endure it.

John 5:14

14 Afterward Jesus found him in the temple and said to him, "Behold, you have become well; do not sin anymore, so that nothing worse happens to you."

John 8:11

11 She said, "No one, LORD." And Jesus said, "I do not condemn you, either. Go. From now on sin no more."

John 8:34-36

34 Jesus answered them, "Truly, truly, I say to you, everyone who commits sin is the slave of sin.
35 The slave does not remain in the house forever; the son does remain forever.
36 So if the Son makes you free, you will be free indeed.

Romans 8:13

13 for if you are living according to the flesh, you must die; but if by the Spirit you are putting to death the deeds of the body, you will live.

Romans 12:21

21 Do not be overcome by evil, but overcome evil with good.

Examples:	Strife	Immorality
	Carousing	Anger
	Impurity	Idolatry
	Envy	Enmity
	Coveting	Jealousy
	Drunkenness	Adultery
	Sorcery	Sensuality

Section Five – The Believer's Rights & Privileges

Fear	Insecurity
Loneliness	Self-loathing
Confusion	Shame
Hopelessness	Despair
Oppression	Vindictiveness
Slander	Gossip
Lust	Pornography
Hatred	
Etc.	

(Not an exhaustive list.)

BE TRANSFORMED BY THE ENTIRE RENEWAL OF YOUR MIND

Romans 12:2

2 And do not be conformed to this world, but be transformed by the renewing of your mind, so that you may prove what the will of God is, that which is good and acceptable and perfect.

Colossians 3:10

10 and have put on the new self who is being renewed to a true knowledge according to the image of the One who created him—

BE GIVEN STRENGTH IN BODY AND SOUL

Isaiah 40:31

31 Yet those who wait for the LORD Will gain new strength;
They will mount up with wings like eagles, they will run and not get tired, they will walk and not become weary

Philippians 4:13

Section Five – The Believer's Rights & Privileges

13 I can do all things through Him who strengthens me.

Hebrews 11:34

34 quenched the power of fire, escaped the edge of the sword, from weakness were made strong, became mighty in war, put foreign armies to flight.

2 Chronicles 16:9

9 For the eyes of the LORD move to and fro throughout the earth that He may strongly support those whose heart is completely His. You have acted foolishly in this. Indeed, from now on you will surely have wars."

Psalm 23:3

3 He restores my soul; He guides me in the paths of righteousness For His name's sake.

Nehemiah 8:10

10 Then he said to them, "Go, eat of the fat, drink of the sweet, and send portions to him who has nothing prepared; for this day is holy to our LORD. Do not be grieved, for the joy of the LORD is your strength."

Psalm 81:1

81 Sing for joy to God our strength; Shout joyfully to the God of Jacob

Psalm 18:32

32 The God who girds me with strength And makes my way blameless?

Psalm 29:11

Section Five – The Believer's Rights & Privileges

11 The LORD will give strength to His people; The LORD will bless His people with peace.

Psalm 37:39

39 But the salvation of the righteous is from the LORD; He is their strength in time of trouble.

Isaiah 41:10

10 'Do not fear, for I am with you; Do not anxiously look about you, for I am your God. I will strengthen you, surely I will help you,
Surely I will uphold you with My righteous right hand.'

Ephesians 3:16

16 that He would grant you, according to the riches of His glory, to be strengthened with power through His Spirit in the inner man,

EXPERIENCE GOOD PHYSICAL HEALTH THROUGH THE POWER OF GOD

Isaiah 53:3-5

3 He was despised and forsaken of men, a man of sorrows and acquainted with grief; And like one from whom men hide their face He was despised, and we did not esteem Him.
4 Surely our pain (grief) He Himself bore, and our sickness (sorrows) He carried; Yet we ourselves esteemed Him stricken, Smitten of God, and afflicted.
5 But He was pierced through for our transgressions, He was crushed for our iniquities; the chastening for our well-being fell upon Him, And by His scourging we are healed.

Pain and sickness are the correct Interpretation of Is. 53:3-5 according to Matthew 8:16-17 below. Pain and sickness are noted

Section Five – The Believer's Rights & Privileges

in the column in the NASB, as alternate translations. I have included them in the above scripture, as I believe this is the correct translation, having studied the writings of Hebrew scholars.

Matthew 8:16-17

16 When evening came, they brought to Him many who were demon-possessed; and He cast out the spirits with a word, and healed all who were ill.
17 This was to fulfill what was spoken through Isaiah the prophet: "He Himself took our infirmities and carried away our diseases."

3 John 2

2 Beloved, I pray that in all respects you may prosper and be in good health, just as your soul prospers.

Exodus 23:25

25 But you shall serve the LORD your God, and He will bless your bread and your water; and I will remove sickness from your midst.

Proverbs 3:7-8

7 Do not be wise in your own eyes; Fear the LORD and turn away from evil.
8 It will be healing to your body and refreshment to your bones.

Proverbs 4:20-22

20 My son, give attention to my words; Incline your ear to my sayings.
21 Do not let them depart from your sight; Keep them in the midst of your heart.
22 For they are life to those who find them And health to all their body.

Psalm 103:1-3

Section Five – The Believer's Rights & Privileges

1 Bless the Lord, O my soul, and all that is within me, bless His holy name.
2 Bless the Lord, O my soul, and forget none of His benefits;
3 Who pardons all your iniquities, Who heals all your diseases;

BE PRAYED FOR BY OTHERS IN ORDER TO BE HEALED

James 5:14-15

14 Is anyone among you sick? Then he must call for the elders of the church and they are to pray over him, anointing him with oil in the name of the LORD;
15 and the prayer offered in faith will restore the one who is sick, and the LORD will raise him up, and if he has committed sins, they will be forgiven him.

PRAY WITH OTHERS IN ORDER FOR THEM TO BE HEALED

Luke 9:1

9 And He called the twelve together, and gave them power and authority over all the demons and to heal diseases.

Luke 10:1 & 8

1 Now after this the Lord appointed seventy others, and sent them in pairs ahead of Him to every city and place where He Himself was going to come.
8 Whatever city you enter and they receive you, eat what is set before you;
9 and heal those in it who are sick, and say to them, 'The kingdom of God has come near to you.'

Mark 16:17-18

Section Five – The Believer's Rights & Privileges

17 These signs will accompany those who have believed: in My name they will cast out demons, they will speak with new tongues;
18 they will pick up serpents, and if they drink any deadly poison, it will not hurt them; they will lay hands on the sick, and they will recover."

Matthew 10:8

8 Heal the sick, raise the dead, cleanse the lepers, cast out demons. Freely you received, freely give.

PRAY FOR OTHERS WHILE ABSENT FROM THEM, IN ORDER FOR THEM TO BE HEALED

John 4:46-54

46 Therefore He came again to Cana of Galilee where He had made the water wine. And there was a royal official whose son was sick at Capernaum.
47 When he heard that Jesus had come out of Judea into Galilee, he went to Him and was imploring Him to come down and heal his son; for he was at the point of death.
48 So Jesus said to him, "Unless you people see signs and wonders, you simply will not believe."
49 The royal official said to Him, "Sir, come down before my child dies."
50 Jesus said to him, "Go; your son lives." The man believed the word that Jesus spoke to him and started off.
51 As he was now going down, his slaves met him, saying that his son was living.
52 So he inquired of them the hour when he began to get better. Then they said to him, "Yesterday at the seventh hour the fever left him."

Section Five – The Believer's Rights & Privileges

53 So the father knew that it was at that hour in which Jesus said to him, "Your son lives"; and he himself believed and his whole household.
54 This is again a second sign that Jesus performed when He had come out of Judea into Galilee.

Matthew 15:22-28

22 And a Canaanite woman from that region came out and began to cry out, saying, "Have mercy on me, LORD, Son of David; my daughter is cruelly demon-possessed."
23 But He did not answer her a word. And His disciples came and implored Him, saying, "Send her away, because she keeps shouting at us."
24 But He answered and said, "I was sent only to the lost sheep of the house of Israel."
25 But she came and began to bow down before Him, saying, "LORD, help me!"
26 And He answered and said, "It is not good to take the children's bread and throw it to the dogs."
27 But she said, "Yes, LORD; but even the dogs feed on the crumbs which fall from their masters' table."
28 Then Jesus said to her, "O woman, your faith is great; it shall be done for you as you wish." And her daughter was healed at once.

BE FREE OF ALL PAIN, DISEASE, WEAKNESS AND INFIRMITY

Psalm 103:2-3

2 Bless the LORD, O my soul, and forget none of His benefits;
3 Who pardons all your iniquities, Who heals all your diseases;

Matthew 4:23

Section Five – The Believer's Rights & Privileges

23 Jesus was going throughout all Galilee, teaching in their synagogues and proclaiming the gospel of the kingdom, and healing every kind of disease and every kind of sickness among the people.

3 John 2

2 Beloved, I pray that in all respects you may prosper and be in good health, just as your soul prospers.

Exodus 23:25

25 But you shall serve the LORD your God, and He will bless your bread and your water; and I will remove sickness from your midst.

Isaiah 53:4a NASB
(See notes in side column of NAS Bible)

4 Surely our sickness He Himself bore, and our pains He carried;

Matthew 8:16-17
Correct translation of Isaiah 53:4a above.

16 When evening came, they brought to Him many who were demon-possessed; and He cast out the spirits with a word, and healed all who were ill.
17 This was to fulfill what was spoken through Isaiah the prophet: "He Himself took our infirmities and carried away our diseases."

Examples:

Blindness	Mark 8:23-25
	Luke 18:35-43
	Psalm 146:8
Deafness	Mark 9:25
Dumbness	Mark 9:17-25
Epilepsy	Matthew 4:24,
	Matthew 17:15-18
Seizures	Mark 9:18-20

Section Five – The Believer's Rights & Privileges

Leprosy	Matthew 8:3
	Matthew 10:8
	Luke 7:22
Hemorrhaging	Mark 5:25-34
Paralysis	Matthew 4:24
	Matthew 9:2
Lameness	Matthew 15:30-31
	Luke 7:22
	Acts 3:2-10, 16
Deformity	Matthew 12:9-13
	Luke 13:11-13
Maiming	Matthew 15:30-31
Torments	Matthew 4:24
Pains	Matthew 4:24
	(Not an exhaustive list.)

BE IMMUNE TO POISONING
AS IN ORAL INGESTION, BITES AND STINGS

Mark 16:17-18

17 These signs will accompany those who have believed: in My name they will cast out demons, they will speak with new tongues;
18 they will pick up serpents, and if they drink any deadly poison, it will not hurt them; they will lay hands on the sick, and they will recover."

BE ABLE TO BEAR CHILDREN- BE FERTILE

Deuteronomy 7:14

14 You shall be blessed above all peoples; there will be no male or female barren among you or among your cattle.

Exodus 23:26

26 There shall be no one miscarrying or barren in your land; I will fulfill the number of your days.

Psalm 113:9

9 He makes the barren woman abide in the house as a joyful mother of children. Praise the LORD!

Psalm 127:3

3 Behold, children are a gift of the LORD, The fruit of the womb is a reward.

Psalm 128:3

3 Your wife shall be like a fruitful vine within your house, your children like olive plants Around your table.

RAISE THE DEAD

Matthew 10:8

8 Heal the sick, raise the dead, cleanse the lepers, cast out demons. Freely you received, freely give.

Luke 7:12-16, 22

12 Now as He approached the gate of the city, a dead man was being carried out, the only son of his mother, and she was a widow; and a sizeable crowd from the city was with her.
13 When the LORD saw her, He felt compassion for her, and said to her, "Do not weep."
14 And He came up and touched the coffin; and the bearers came to a halt. And He said, "Young man, I say to you, arise!"
15 The dead man sat up and began to speak. And Jesus gave him back to his mother.

Section Five – The Believer's Rights & Privileges

16 Fear gripped them all, and they began glorifying God, saying, "A great prophet has arisen among us!" and, "God has visited His people!"

22 And He answered and said to them, "Go and report to John what you have seen and heard: the blind receive sight, the lame walk, the lepers are cleansed, and the deaf hear, the dead are raised up, the poor have the gospel preached to them.

John 11:44

44 The man who had died came forth, bound hand and foot with wrappings, and his face was wrapped around with a cloth. Jesus said to them, "Unbind him, and let him go."

John 14:12-14

12 Truly, truly, I say to you, he who believes in Me, the works that I do, he will do also; and greater works than these he will do; because I go to the Father.
13 Whatever you ask in My name, that will I do, so that the Father may be glorified in the Son.
14 If you ask Me anything in My name, I will do it.

BE FREE FROM DEMONS
UNCLEAN/EVIL SPIRITS

Mark 5:1-13

1 They came to the other side of the sea, into the country of the Gerasenes.
2 When He got out of the boat, immediately a man from the tombs with an unclean spirit met Him,
3 and he had his dwelling among the tombs. And no one was able to bind him anymore, even with a chain;
4 because he had often been bound with shackles and chains, and the chains had been torn apart by him and

Section Five – The Believer's Rights & Privileges

the shackles broken in pieces, and no one was strong enough to subdue him.
5 Constantly, night and day, he was screaming among the tombs and in the mountains, and gashing himself with stones.
6 Seeing Jesus from a distance, he ran up and bowed down before Him;
7 and shouting with a loud voice, he said, "What business do we have with each other, Jesus, Son of the Most High God? I implore You by God, do not torment me!"
8 For He had been saying to him, "Come out of the man, you unclean spirit!"
9 And He was asking him, "What is your name?" And he said to Him, "My name is Legion; for we are many."
10 And he began to implore Him earnestly not to send them out of the country.
11 Now there was a large herd of swine feeding nearby on the mountain.
12 The demons implored Him, saying, "Send us into the swine so that we may enter them."
13 Jesus gave them permission. And coming out, the unclean spirits entered the swine; and the herd rushed down the steep bank into the sea, about two thousand of them; and they were drowned in the sea.

Luke 9:1

9 And He called the twelve together, and gave them power and authority over all the demons and to heal diseases.

Matthew 10:8

8 Heal the sick, raise the dead, cleanse the lepers, cast out demons. Freely you received, freely give.

John 14:12-14

Section Five – The Believer's Rights & Privileges

12 Truly, truly, I say to you, he who believes in Me, the works that I do, he will do also; and greater works than these he will do; because I go to the Father.
13 Whatever you ask in My name, that will I do, so that the Father may be glorified in the Son.
14 If you ask Me anything in My name, I will do it.

HAVE AUTHORITY OVER UNCLEAN SPIRITS IN OTHERS

Mark 16:17-18

17 These signs will accompany those who have believed: in My name they will cast out demons, they will speak with new tongues;
18 they will pick up serpents, and if they drink any deadly poison, it will not hurt them; they will lay hands on the sick, and they will recover."

Luke 9:1

9 And He called the twelve together, and gave them power and authority over all the demons and to heal diseases.

Acts 16:16-18

16 It happened that as we were going to the place of prayer, a slave-girl having a spirit of divination met us, who was bringing her masters much profit by fortune-telling.
17 Following after Paul and us, she kept crying out, saying, "These men are bond-servants of the Most High God, who are proclaiming to you the way of salvation."
18 She continued doing this for many days. But Paul was greatly annoyed, and turned and said to the spirit, "I command you in the name of Jesus Christ to come out of her!" And it came out at that very moment.

Section Five – The Believer's Rights & Privileges

PERFORM SIGNS, WONDERS, MIRACLES AND HEALING, IN THE NAME OF JESUS CHRIST

Acts 14:3

3 Therefore they spent a long time there speaking boldly with reliance upon the LORD, who was testifying to the word of His grace, granting that signs and wonders be done by their hands.

Mark 16:17-18

17 These signs will accompany those who have believed: in My name they will cast out demons, they will speak with new tongues;
18 they will pick up serpents, and if they drink any deadly poison, it will not hurt them; they will lay hands on the sick, and they will recover."

Acts 3:6, 16

6 But Peter said, "I do not possess silver and gold, but what I do have I give to you: In the name of Jesus Christ the Nazarene—walk!"

16 And on the basis of faith in His name, it is the name of Jesus which has strengthened this man whom you see and know; and the faith which comes through Him has given him this perfect health in the presence of you all.

Acts 4:10

10 let it be known to all of you and to all the people of Israel, that by the name of Jesus Christ the Nazarene, whom you crucified, whom God raised from the dead—

Section Five – The Believer's Rights & Privileges

by this name this man stands here before you in good health.

Acts 4:30

30 while You extend Your hand to heal, and signs and wonders take place through the name of Your holy servant Jesus."

Acts 8:5-8

5 Philip went down to the city of Samaria and began proclaiming Christ to them.
6 The crowds with one accord were giving attention to what was said by Philip, as they heard and saw the signs which he was performing.
7 For in the case of many who had unclean spirits, they were coming out of them shouting with a loud voice; and many who had been paralyzed and lame were healed.
8 So there was much rejoicing in that city.

HAVE YOUR DAILY, PHYSICAL NEEDS MET

Matthew 6:25-33

25 "For this reason I say to you, do not be worried about your life, as to what you will eat or what you will drink; nor for your body, as to what you will put on. Is not life more than food, and the body more than clothing?
26 Look at the birds of the air, that they do not sow, nor reap nor gather into barns, and yet your heavenly Father feeds them. Are you not worth much more than they?
27 And who of you by being worried can add a single hour to his life?

Section Five – The Believer's Rights & Privileges

28 And why are you worried about clothing? Observe how the lilies of the field grow; they do not toil nor do they spin,
29 yet I say to you that not even Solomon in all his glory clothed himself like one of these.
30 But if God so clothes the grass of the field, which is alive today and tomorrow is thrown into the furnace, will He not much more clothe you? You of little faith!
31 Do not worry then, saying, 'What will we eat?' or 'What will we drink?' or 'What will we wear for clothing?'
32 For the Gentiles eagerly seek all these things; for your heavenly Father knows that you need all these things.
33 But seek first His kingdom and His righteousness, and all these things will be added to you.

Psalm 146:7

7 Who executes justice for the oppressed; Who gives food to the hungry. The LORD sets the prisoners free.

Psalm 145:15-16

15 The eyes of all look to You, And You give them their food in due time.
16 You open Your hand And satisfy the desire of every living thing

EVEN IF IT REQUIRES A MIRACLE

Matthew 14:15-21

15 When it was evening, the disciples came to Him and said, "This place is desolate and the hour is already late; so send the crowds away, that they may go into the villages and buy food for themselves."
16 But Jesus said to them, "They do not need to go away; you give them something to eat!"

Section Five – The Believer's Rights & Privileges

17 They said to Him, "We have here only five loaves and two fish."
18 And He said, "Bring them here to Me."
19 Ordering the people to sit down on the grass, He took the five loaves and the two fish, and looking up toward heaven, He blessed the food, and breaking the loaves He gave them to the disciples, and the disciples gave them to the crowds,
20 and they all ate and were satisfied. They picked up what was left over of the broken pieces, twelve full baskets.
21 There were about five thousand men who ate, besides women and children.

Matthew 15:32-38

32 And Jesus called His disciples to Him, and said, "I feel compassion for the people, because they have remained with Me now three days and have nothing to eat; and I do not want to send them away hungry, for they might faint on the way."
33 The disciples said to Him, "Where would we get so many loaves in this desolate place to satisfy such a large crowd?"
34 And Jesus said to them, "How many loaves do you have?" And they said, "Seven, and a few small fish."
35 And He directed the people to sit down on the ground;
36 and He took the seven loaves and the fish; and giving thanks, He broke them and started giving them to the disciples, and the disciples gave them to the people.
37 And they all ate and were satisfied, and they picked up what was left over of the broken pieces, seven large baskets full.
38 And those who ate were four thousand men, besides women and children.

1 Kings 17:4-24

Section Five – The Believer's Rights & Privileges

4 It shall be that you will drink of the brook, and I have commanded the ravens to provide for you there."
5 So he went and did according to the word of the LORD, for he went and lived by the brook Cherith, which is east of the Jordan.
6 The ravens brought him bread and meat in the morning and bread and meat in the evening, and he would drink from the brook.
7 It happened after a while that the brook dried up, because there was no rain in the.
8 Then the word of the LORD came to him, saying,
9 "Arise, go to Zarephath, which belongs to Sidon, and stay there; behold, I have commanded a widow there to provide for you."
10 So he arose and went to Zarephath, and when he came to the gate of the city, behold, a widow was there gathering sticks; and he called to her and said, "Please get me a little water in a jar, that I may drink."
11 As she was going to get it, he called to her and said, "Please bring me a piece of bread in your hand."
12 But she said, "As the LORD your God lives, I have no bread, only a handful of flour in the bowl and a little oil in the jar; and behold, I am gathering a few sticks that I may go in and prepare for me and my son, that we may eat it and die."
13 Then Elijah said to her, "Do not fear; go, do as you have said, but make me a little bread cake from it first and bring it out to me, and afterward you may make one for yourself and for your son.
14 For thus says the LORD God of Israel, 'The bowl of flour shall not be exhausted, nor shall the jar of oil be empty, until the day that the LORD sends rain on the face of the earth.'"
15 So she went and did according to the word of Elijah, and she and he and her household ate for many days.
16 The bowl of flour was not exhausted nor did the jar of oil become empty, according to the word of the LORD which He spoke through Elijah.
17 Now it came about after these things that the son of the woman, the mistress of the house, became sick;

Section Five – The Believer's Rights & Privileges

and his sickness was so severe that there was no breath left in him.
18 So she said to Elijah, "What do I have to do with you, O man of God? You have come to me to bring my iniquity to remembrance and to put my son to death!"
19 He said to her, "Give me your son." Then he took him from her bosom and carried him up to the upper room where he was living, and laid him on his own bed.
20 He called to the LORD and said, "O LORD my God, have You also brought calamity to the widow with whom I am staying, by causing her son to die?"
21 Then he stretched himself upon the child three times, and called to the LORD and said, "O LORD my God, I pray You, let this child's life return to him."
22 The LORD heard the voice of Elijah, and the life of the child to him and he revived.
23 Elijah took the child and brought him down from the upper room into the house and gave him to his mother; and Elijah said, "See, your son is alive."
24 Then the woman said to Elijah, "Now I know that you are a man of God and that the word of the LORD in your mouth is truth."

Jonah 4:6

6 So the LORD God appointed a plant and it grew up over Jonah to be a shade over his head to deliver him from his discomfort. And Jonah was extremely happy about the plant.

HAVE LIFE, AND THAT MORE ABUNDANTLY

John 10:10

10 The thief comes only to steal and kill and destroy; I came that they may have life, and have it abundantly.

John 5:24

Section Five – The Believer's Rights & Privileges

24 "Truly, truly, I say to you, he who hears My word, and believes Him who sent Me, has eternal life, and does not come into judgment, but has passed out of death into life.

1 John 3:14

14 We know that we have passed out of death into life, because we love the brethren. He who does not love abides in death.

BE FREE FROM POVERTY

Deuteronomy 28:11-12

11 The LORD will make you abound in prosperity, in the offspring of your body and in the offspring of your beast and in the produce of your ground, in the land which the LORD swore to your fathers to give you.
12 The LORD will open for you His good storehouse, the heavens, to give rain to your land in its season and to bless all the work of your hand; and you shall lend to many nations, but you shall not borrow.

Deuteronomy 15:4

4 However, there will be no poor among you, since the LORD will surely bless you in the land which the LORD your God is giving you as an inheritance to possess,

Luke 7:22

22 And He answered and said to them, "Go and report to John what you have seen and heard: the blind receive sight, the lame walk, the lepers are cleansed, and the deaf hear, the dead are raised up, the poor have the gospel preached to them.

Isaiah 1:19

19 "If you consent and obey, You will eat the best of the land;

HAVE YOUR SILVER AND GOLD INCREASE

Genesis 24:35

35 The LORD has greatly blessed my master, so that he has become rich; and He has given him flocks and herds, and silver and gold, and servants and maids, and camels and donkeys.

Genesis 13:2

2 Now Abram was very rich in livestock, in silver and in gold.

Deuteronomy 8:13

13 and when your herds and your flocks multiply, and your silver and gold multiply, and all that you have multiplies,

HAVE ALL THAT YOU POSSESS MULTIPLIED

Deuteronomy 8:13

13 and when your herds and your flocks multiply, and your silver and gold multiply, and all that you have multiplies,

BE MADE RICH

Proverbs 10:22

Section Five – The Believer's Rights & Privileges

22 It is the blessing of the LORD that makes rich, And He adds no sorrow to it.

Proverbs 8:18

18 "Riches and honor are with me, Enduring wealth and righteousness.

Proverbs 14:24

24 The crown of the wise is their riches, but the folly of fools is foolishness.

Proverbs 22:4

4 The reward of humility and the fear of the LORD are riches, honor and life.

Psalm 112:3

3 Wealth and riches are in his house, and his righteousness endures forever.

Proverbs 24:4

4 And by knowledge the rooms are filled with all precious and pleasant riches.

Isaiah 30:23

23 Then He will give you rain for the seed which you will sow in the ground, and bread from the yield of the ground, and it will be rich and plenteous; on that day your livestock will graze in a roomy pasture.

Isaiah 61:6

6 But you will be called the priests of the LORD; You will be spoken of as ministers of our God. You will eat the wealth of nations, and in their riches you will boast.

Section Five – The Believer's Rights & Privileges

Genesis 26:12

12 Now Isaac sowed in that land and reaped in the same year a hundredfold. And the LORD blessed him,

Ecclesiastes 5:19

19 Furthermore, as for every man to whom God has given riches and wealth, He has also empowered him to eat from them and to receive his reward and rejoice in his labor; this is the gift of God.

2 Corinthians 8:9

9 For you know the grace of our LORD Jesus Christ, that though He was rich, yet for your sake He became poor, so that you through His poverty might become rich.

1 Timothy 6:17

17 Instruct those who are rich in this present world not to be conceited or to fix their hope on the uncertainty of riches, but on God, who richly supplies us with all things to enjoy.

GAIN ENDURING WEALTH

Deuteronomy 8:17-18

17 Otherwise, you may say in your heart, 'My power and the strength of my hand made me this wealth.'
18 But you shall remember the LORD your God, for it is He who is giving you power to make wealth, that He may confirm His covenant which He swore to your fathers, as it is this day.

Psalm 112:3

Section Five – The Believer's Rights & Privileges

3 Wealth and riches are in his house, and his righteousness endures forever.

Proverbs 3:9

9 Honor the LORD from your wealth and from the first of all your produce;

Proverbs 8:18-21

18 "Riches and honor are with me, Enduring wealth and righteousness.
19 "My fruit is better than gold, even pure gold, and my yield better than choicest silver.
20 "I walk in the way of righteousness, in the midst of the paths of justice,
21 To endow those who love me with wealth, that I may fill their treasuries.

Proverbs 13:22

22 A good man leaves an inheritance to his children's children,
And the wealth of the sinner is stored up for the righteous.

Proverbs 15:6

6 Great wealth is in the house of the righteous, but trouble is in the income of the wicked.

Isaiah 60:5

5 "Then you will see and be radiant, And your heart will thrill and rejoice; Because the abundance of the sea will be turned to you, The wealth of the nations will come to you.

Isaiah 60:11

11 "Your gates will be open continually; They will not be closed day or night, So that men may bring to you

the wealth of the nations, With their kings led in procession.

Isaiah 61:6

6 But you will be called the priests of the LORD; you will be spoken of as ministers of our God. You will eat the wealth of nations, and in their riches you will boast.

HAVE FORTUNES RESTORED

Jeremiah 32:44

44 Men will buy fields for money, sign and seal deeds, and call in witnesses in the land of Benjamin, in the environs of Jerusalem, in the cities of Judah, in the cities of the hill country, in the cities of the lowland and in the cities of the Negev; for I will restore their fortunes,' declares the LORD."

Jeremiah 33:11

11 the voice of joy and the voice of gladness, the voice of the bridegroom and the voice of the bride, the voice of those who say, "Give thanks to the LORD of hosts, For the LORD is good, For His lovingkindness is everlasting"; and of those who bring a thank offering into the house of the LORD. For I will restore the fortunes of the land as they were at first,' says the LORD.

Hosea 6:11

11 Also, O Judah, there is a harvest appointed for you, When I restore the fortunes of My people.

Zephaniah 3:20

Section Five – The Believer's Rights & Privileges

20 "At that time I will bring you in, Even at the time when I gather you together; Indeed, I will give you renown and praise Among all the peoples of the earth, When I restore your fortunes before your eyes," Says the LORD.

Job 42:10

10 The LORD restored the fortunes of Job when he prayed for his friends, and the LORD increased all that Job had twofold.

Joel 3:1

3 For behold, in those days and at that time, when I restore the fortunes of Judah and Jerusalem

---

ABOUND IN PROSPERITY

Psalm 37:11

11 But the humble will inherit the land and will delight themselves in abundant prosperity.

3 John 1:2

2 Beloved, I pray that in all respects you may prosper and be in good health, just as your soul prospers.

Philippians 4:19

19 And my God will supply all your needs according to His riches in glory in Christ Jesus.

Deuteronomy 30:19

19 I call heaven and earth to witness against you today, that I have set before you life and death, the blessing and the curse. So choose life in order that you may live, you and your descendants,

Section Five – The Believer's Rights & Privileges

Deuteronomy 8:18

18 But you shall remember the LORD your God, for it is He who is giving you power to make wealth, that He may confirm His covenant which He swore to your fathers, as it is this day.

Deuteronomy 28:11

11 The LORD will make you abound in prosperity, in the offspring of your body and in the offspring of your beast and in the produce of your ground, in the land which the LORD swore to your fathers to give you.

2 Chronicles 26:5

5 He continued to seek God in the days of Zechariah, who had understanding through the vision of God; and as long as he sought the LORD, God prospered him.

Joshua 1:8

8 This book of the law shall not depart from your mouth, but you shall meditate on it day and night, so that you may be careful to do according to all that is written in it; for then you will make your way prosperous, and then you will have success.

Job 36:11

11 "If they hear and serve Him, They will end their days in prosperity and their years in pleasures.

Psalm 1:3

3 He will be like a tree firmly planted by streams of water, which yields its fruit in its season and its leaf does not wither; and in whatever he does, he prospers.

Psalm 25:13

Section Five – The Believer's Rights & Privileges

13 His soul will abide in prosperity, and his descendants will inherit the land.

Psalm 34:10

10 The young lions do lack and suffer hunger; but they who seek the LORD shall not be in want of any good thing.

Psalm 35:27b

27 Let them shout for joy and rejoice, who favor my vindication; and let them say continually, "The LORD be magnified, Who delights in the prosperity of His servant."

Psalm 68:6

6 God makes a home for the lonely; He leads out the prisoners into prosperity, only the rebellious dwell in a parched land.

Psalm 84:11

11 For the LORD God is a sun and shield; The LORD gives grace and glory; No good thing does He withhold from those who walk uprightly.

Proverbs 8:20-21

20 "I walk in the way of righteousness, In the midst of the paths of justice,
21 To endow those who love me with wealth, that I may fill their treasuries.

Proverbs 13:21

21 Adversity pursues sinners, but the righteous will be rewarded with prosperity.

Section Five – The Believer's Rights & Privileges

Proverbs 11:25

25 The generous man will be prosperous, and he who waters will himself be watered.

BE FREE OF ALL LACK

Deuteronomy 8:9

9 a land where you will eat food without scarcity, in which you will not lack anything; a land whose stones are iron, and out of whose hills you can dig copper.

Judges 18:10

10 When you enter, you will come to a secure people with a spacious land; for God has given it into your hand, a place where there is no lack of anything that is on the earth."

HAVE GOD BLESS EVERYTHING YOU PUT YOUR HAND TO

Deuteronomy 28:8

8 The LORD will command the blessing upon you in your barns and in all that you put your hand to, and He will bless you in the land which the LORD your God gives you.

BE BLESSED WITH ABRAHAM THE BELIEVER

Galatians 3:9-14

9 So then those who are of faith are blessed with Abraham, the believer.

Section Five – The Believer's Rights & Privileges

10 For as many as are of the works of the Law are under a curse; for it is written, "Cursed is everyone who does not abide by all things written in the book of the law, to perform them."
11 Now that no one is justified by the Law before God is evident; for, "The righteous man shall live by faith."
12 However, the Law is not of faith; on the contrary, "He who practices them shall live by them."
13 Christ redeemed us from the curse of the Law, having become a curse for us—for it is written, "Cursed is everyone who hangs on a tree"—
14 in order that in Christ Jesus the blessing of Abraham might come to the Gentiles, so that we would receive the promise of the Spirit through faith.

Genesis 12:2-3

2 And I will make you a great nation, and I will bless you, and make your name great; And so you shall be a blessing;
3 And I will bless those who bless you, and the one who curses you I will curse. And in you all the families of the earth will be blessed."

Genesis 18:18

18 since Abraham will surely become a great and mighty nation, and in him all the nations of the earth will be blessed?

Genesis 22:18

18 In your seed all the nations of the earth shall be blessed, because you have obeyed My voice."

Genesis 24:1

24 Now Abraham was old, advanced in age; and the LORD had blessed Abraham in every way.

Genesis 28:14

Section Five – The Believer's Rights & Privileges

14 Your descendants will also be like the dust of the earth, and you will spread out to the west and to the east and to the north and to the south; and in you and in your descendants shall all the families of the earth be blessed.

ENJOY ALL THE BLESSINGS OF GOD

Deuteronomy 11:26-27

26 "See, I am setting before you today a blessing and a curse:
27 the blessing, if you listen to the commandments of the LORD your God, which I am commanding you today;

Deuteronomy 28:2

2 All these blessings will come upon you and overtake you if you obey the LORD your God:

Deuteronomy 30:19

19 I call heaven and earth to witness against you today, that I have set before you life and death, the blessing and the curse. So choose life in order that you may live, you and your descendants,

Psalm 24:1-5

1 The earth is the LORD's, and all it contains, the world, and those who dwell in it.
2 For He has founded it upon the seas and established it upon the rivers.
3 Who may ascend into the hill of the LORD? And who may stand in His holy place?
4 He who has clean hands and a pure heart, who has not lifted up his soul to falsehood and has not sworn deceitfully.

Section Five – The Believer's Rights & Privileges

5 He shall receive a blessing from the LORD and righteousness from the God of his salvation.

Psalm 109:17

17 He also loved cursing, so it came to him; and he did not delight in blessing, so it was far from him.

Proverbs 11:11

11 By the blessing of the upright a city is exalted, but by the mouth of the wicked it is torn down.

Proverbs 28:20

20 A faithful man will abound with blessings, but he who makes haste to be rich will not go unpunished.

Isaiah 44:3

3 'For I will pour out water on the thirsty land And streams on the dry ground; I will pour out My Spirit on your offspring And My blessing on your descendants;

Acts 13:34

34 As for the fact that He raised Him up from the dead, no longer to return to decay, He has spoken in this way: 'I will give you the holy and sure blessings of David.'

Romans 4:6

6 just as David also speaks of the blessing on the man to whom God credits righteousness apart from works:

Ephesians 1:3

3 Blessed be the God and Father of our LORD Jesus Christ, who has blessed us with every spiritual blessing in the heavenly places in Christ,

Section Five – The Believer's Rights & Privileges

BECOME A BLESSING AND BLESS OTHERS

Galatians 3:13-14

13 Christ redeemed us from the curse of the Law, having become a curse for us—for it is written, "Cursed is everyone who hangs on a tree"—
14 in order that in Christ Jesus the blessing of Abraham might come to the Gentiles, so that we would receive the promise of the Spirit through faith.

Genesis 12:2-3

2 And I will make you a great nation, and I will bless you, and make your name great; and so you shall be a blessing;
3 And I will bless those who bless you, and the one who curses you I will curse. And in you all the families of the earth will be blessed."

Matthew 10:13

13 If the house is worthy, give it your blessing of peace. But if it is not worthy, take back your blessing of peace.

Zechariah 8:13

13 It will come about that just as you were a curse among the nations, O house of Judah and house of Israel, so I will save you that you may become a blessing. Do not fear; let your hands be strong.'

James 3:10

10 from the same mouth come both blessing and cursing. My brethren, these things ought not to be this way.

Section Five – The Believer's Rights & Privileges

1 Peter 3:9

9 not returning evil for evil or insult for insult, but giving a blessing instead; for you were called for the very purpose that you might inherit a blessing.

BE SUPERNATURALLY BLESSED BY GOD, IN THE CITY, OR IN THE COUNTRY

Deuteronomy 28:3, 10

3 "Blessed shall you be in the city, and blessed shall you be in the country.

10 So all the peoples of the earth will see that you are called by the name of the LORD, and they will be afraid of you.

Malachi 3:12

12 "All the nations will call you blessed, for you shall be a delightful land," says the LORD of hosts.

HAVE SUCCESS IN ALL YOUR ENDEAVORS

Deuteronomy 8:18

18 But you shall remember the LORD your God, for it is He who is giving you power to make wealth, that He may confirm His covenant which He swore to your fathers, as it is this day.

Deuteronomy 14:29

29 so that the Levites (who have no allotment or inheritance of their own) and the aliens, the fatherless and the widows who live in your towns may come and

Section Five – The Believer's Rights & Privileges

eat and be satisfied, and so that the LORD your God may bless you in all the work of your hands.

Deuteronomy 15:10

10 "You shall generously give to him, and your heart shall not be grieved when you give to him, because for this thing the LORD your God will bless you in all your work and in all your undertakings.

Psalm 1:3

3 He will be like a tree firmly planted by streams water, Which yields its fruit in its season And its leaf does not wither; And in whatever he does, he prospers.

Deuteronomy 28:8

8 The LORD will command the blessing upon you in your barns and in all that you put your hand to, and He will bless you in the land which the LORD your God gives you.

Psalm 90:17

17 Let the favor of the LORD our God be upon us; and confirm for us the work of our hands; Yes, confirm the work of our hands.

BE GIVEN THE DESIRES OF YOUR HEART

Psalm 37:4

4 Delight yourself in the LORD; And He will give you the desires of your heart.

Mark 11:24 KJV

Therefore I say unto you, what things soever ye desire, when ye pray, believe that ye receive them, and ye shall have them.

Section Five – The Believer's Rights & Privileges

INHERIT LAND

Psalm 37:11

11 But the humble will inherit the land and will delight themselves in abundant prosperity.

Psalm 105:44

44 He gave them also the lands of the nations, that they might take possession of the fruit of the peoples' labor,

Jeremiah 12:15

15 And it will come about that after I have uprooted them, I will again have compassion on them; and I will bring them back, each one to his inheritance and each one to his land.

Deuteronomy 28:8

8 The LORD will command the blessing upon you in your barns and in all that you put your hand to, and He will bless you in the land which the LORD your God gives you.

Psalm 37:9, 11, 34

9 For evildoers will be cut off, but those who wait for the LORD, they will inherit the land.

11 But the humble will inherit the land and will delight themselves in abundant prosperity.

34 Wait for the LORD and keep His way, and He will exalt you to inherit the land; when the wicked are cut off, you will see it.

Section Five – The Believer's Rights & Privileges

POSSESS A HOME FILLED WITH ALL PRECIOUS AND PLEASANT RICHES

Proverbs 24:3-4

3 By wisdom a house is built, and by understanding it is established;
4 And by knowledge the rooms are filled with all precious and pleasant riches.

Proverbs 8:21

21 To endow those who love me with wealth, that I may fill their treasuries.

Nehemiah 9:25

25 "They captured fortified cities and a fertile land. They took possession of houses full of every good thing, Hew cisterns, vineyards, olive groves, fruit trees in abundance. So they ate, were filled and grew fat, And reveled in Your great goodness.

Mark 10:30

30 but that he will receive a hundred times as much now in he present age, houses and brothers and sisters and mothers and children and farms, along with persecutions; and in the age to come, eternal life.

ENJOY PROTECTION FOR YOUR HOME

Job 5:24

24 "You will know that your tent is secure, for you will visit your abode and fear no loss.

Psalm 4:8

8 In peace I will both lie down and sleep, for You alone, O LORD, make me to dwell in safety.

HAVE NECESSARY RAIN IN ITS SEASON
FREEDOM FROM DROUGHT

Deuteronomy 28:12

12 The LORD will open for you His good storehouse, the heavens, to give rain to your land in its season and to bless all the work of your hand; and you shall lend to many nations, but you shall not borrow.

Leviticus 26:4

4 then I shall give you rains in their season, so that the land will yield its produce and the trees of the field will bear their fruit.

Deuteronomy 11:14

14 that He will give the rain for your land in its season, the early and late rain, that you may gather in your grain and your new wine and your oil.

Job 5:10

10 "He gives rain on the earth And sends water on the fields,

Jeremiah 5:24

24 'They do not say in their heart, "Let us now fear the LORD our God, Who gives rain in its season, Both the autumn rain and the spring rain, Who keeps for us The appointed weeks of the harvest."

Amos 4:7

Section Five – The Believer's Rights & Privileges

7 "Furthermore, I withheld the rain from you while there were still three months until harvest. Then I would send rain on one city and on another city I would not send rain; One part would be rained on, While the part not rained on would dry up.

HAVE PRODUCTIVE CROPS

Deuteronomy 28:8-11

8 The LORD will command the blessing upon you in your barns and in all that you put your hand to, and He will bless you in the land which the LORD your God gives you.
9 The LORD will establish you as a holy people to Himself, as He swore to you, if you keep the commandments of the LORD your God and walk in His ways.
10 So all the peoples of the earth will see that you are called by the name of the LORD, and they will be afraid of you.
11 The LORD will make you abound in prosperity, in the offspring of your body and in the offspring of your beast and in the produce of your ground, in the land which the LORD swore to your fathers to give you.

Malachi 3:11

11 Then I will rebuke the devourer for you, so that it will not destroy the fruits of the ground; nor will your vine in the field cast its grapes," says the LORD of hosts.

HAVE ABUNDANCE
EVEN IN DAYS OF FAMINE

Job 5:20

Section Five – The Believer's Rights & Privileges

20 "In famine He will redeem you from death, And in war from the power of the sword.

Psalm 33:19

19 To deliver their soul from death And to keep them alive in famine.

Psalm 37:19

19 They will not be ashamed in the time of evil, And in the days of famine they will have abundance.

HAVE FRUIT TREES PRODUCE A GOOD YIELD

Ezekiel 34:27

27 Also the tree of the field will yield its fruit and the earth will yield its increase, and they will be secure on their land. Then they will know that I am the LORD, when I have broken the bars of their yoke and have delivered them from the hand of those who enslaved them.

TAKE AUTHORITY OVER WEATHER AND ELEMENTS

WATER – WIND - RAIN

Matthew 14:28-29

28 Peter said to Him, "LORD, if it is You, command me to come to You on the water."
29 And He said, "Come!" And Peter got out of the boat, and walked on the water and came toward Jesus.

Mark 4:39-40

Section Five – The Believer's Rights & Privileges

39 And He got up and rebuked the wind and said to the sea, "Hush, be still." And the wind died down and it became perfectly calm.
40 And He said to them, "Why are you afraid? Do you still have no faith?"

James 5:17-18

17 Elijah was a man with a nature like ours, and he prayed earnestly that it would not rain, and it did not rain on the earth for three years and six months.
18 Then he prayed again, and the sky poured rain and the earth produced its fruit.

EARTH

Mark 11:23

23 Truly I say to you, whoever says to this mountain, 'Be taken up and cast into the sea,' and does not doubt in his heart, but believes that what he says is going to happen, it will be granted him.

HAVE HARMFUL BEASTS ELIMINATED FROM YOUR LAND

Ezekiel 34:25

25 "I will make a covenant of peace with them and eliminate harmful beasts from the land so that they may live securely in the wilderness and sleep in the woods.

BE PROTECTED FROM WILD BEASTS

Job 5:22-23

22 "You will laugh at violence and famine, And you will not be afraid of wild beasts.
23 "For you will be in league with the stones of the field, and the beasts of the field will be at peace with you.

HAVE PROTECTION FOR YOUR ANIMALS

Psalm 36:6

6 Your righteousness is like the mountains of God; Your judgments are like a great deep. O LORD, You preserve man and beast.

HAVE SAFETY FROM (AND VICTORY OVER) ENEMIES

Psalm 138:7

7 Though I walk in the midst of trouble, You will revive me; You will stretch forth Your hand against the wrath of my enemies, And Your right hand will save me.

Malachi 4:3

3 You will tread down the wicked, for they will be ashes under the soles of your feet on the day which I am preparing," says the LORD of hosts.

Deuteronomy 28:7

7 "The LORD shall cause your enemies who rise up against you to be defeated before you; they will come out against you one way and will flee before you seven ways.

Section Five – The Believer's Rights & Privileges

BE PROTECTED FROM ALL EVIL

Psalm 121:7

7 The LORD will protect you from all evil; He will keep your soul.

Psalm 32:7

7 You are my hiding place; You preserve me from trouble; You surround me with songs of deliverance. Selah.

BE RESCUED

Psalm 34:7

7 The angel of the LORD encamps around those who fear Him, And rescues them.

BE PROTECTED IN WAR

Job 5:20

20 "In famine He will redeem you from death, And in war from the power of the sword.

BE PROTECTED BY ANGELS

Psalm 34:7

7 The angel of the LORD encamps around those who fear Him, and rescues them.

Psalm 91:11

11 For He will give His angels charge concerning you, to guard you in all your ways.

Section Five – The Believer's Rights & Privileges

Psalm 103:20

20 Bless the LORD, you His angels, Mighty in strength, who perform His word, Obeying the voice of His word!

Acts 12:5-11

5 So Peter was kept in the prison, but prayer for him was being made fervently by the church to God.
6 On the very night when Herod was about to bring him forward, Peter was sleeping between two soldiers, bound with two chains, and guards in front of the door were watching over the prison.
7 And behold, an angel of the Lord suddenly appeared and a light shone in the cell; and he struck Peter's side and woke him up, saying, "Get up quickly." And his chains fell off his hands.
8 And the angel said to him, "Gird yourself and put on your sandals." And he did so. And he said to him, "Wrap your cloak around you and follow me."
9 And he went out and continued to follow, and he did not know that what was being done by the angel was real, but thought he was seeing a vision.
10 When they had passed the first and second guard, they came to the iron gate that leads into the city, which opened for them by itself; and they went out and went along one street, and immediately the angel departed from him. 11 When Peter came to himself, he said, "Now I know for sure that the Lord has sent forth His angel and rescued me from the hand of Herod and from all that the Jewish people were expecting."

Hebrews 1:14

14 Are they not all ministering spirits, sent out to render service for the sake of those who will inherit salvation?

BE PROTECTED FROM THE WORDS OF OTHERS

Job 5:15, 21

15 "But He saves from the sword of their mouth, and the poor from the hand of the mighty.
21 "You will be hidden from the scourge of the tongue, and you will not be afraid of violence when it comes.

Psalm 31:20

20 You hide them in the secret place of Your presence from the conspiracies of man; You keep them secretly in a shelter from the strife of tongues.

BE PRESERVED, SAVED, DELIVERED FROM TROUBLE OR EVIL

Psalm 32:7

7 You are my hiding place; You preserve me from trouble; You surround me with songs of deliverance. Selah.

Psalm 31:23

23 O love the LORD, all you His godly ones! The LORD preserves the faithful and fully recompenses the proud doer.

Psalm 145:20

20 The LORD keeps all who love Him, But all the wicked He will destroy.

Psalm 121:7

7 The LORD will protect you from all evil; He will keep your soul.

Section Five – The Believer's Rights & Privileges

Psalm 34:6, 17

6 This poor man cried, and the LORD heard him And saved him out of all his troubles.

BE DELIVERED FROM THE AFFLICTION OF THOSE WHO ARE STRONGER THAN YOU

Psalm 35:10

10 All my bones will say, "LORD, who is like You, Who delivers the afflicted from him who is too strong for him, and the afflicted and the needy from him who robs him?"

Psalm 9:9

9 The LORD also will be a stronghold for the oppressed, A stronghold in times of trouble;

Psalm 18:17

17 He delivered me from my strong enemy, And from those who hated me, for they were too mighty for me.

Psalm 12:5

5 "Because of the devastation of the afflicted, because of the groaning of the needy, Now I will arise," says the LORD; "I will set him in the safety for which he longs."

BE FREE OF FEAR

2 Timothy 1:7 (KJV)

Section Five – The Believer's Rights & Privileges

7 For God has not given us a spirit of fear, but of power and of love and of a sound mind.

1 John 4:17-18

17 By this, love is perfected with us, so that we may have confidence in the day of judgment; because as He is, so also are we in this world.
18 There is no fear in love; but perfect love casts out fear, because fear involves punishment, and the one who fears is not perfected in love.

Isaiah 41:10

10 'Do not fear, for I am with you; Do not anxiously look about you, for I am your God. I will strengthen you, surely I will help you, surely I will uphold you with My righteous right hand.'

Psalm 23:4

4 Even though I walk through the valley of the shadow of death, I fear no evil, for You are with me; Your rod and Your staff, they comfort me.

Proverbs 3:24

24 When you lie down, you will not be afraid; When you lie down, your sleep will be sweet.

NOT FEAR VIOLENCE WHEN IT COMES

Job 5:21

21 "You will be hidden from the scourge of the tongue, and you will not be afraid of violence when it comes.

Section Five – The Believer's Rights & Privileges

HAVE PEACEFUL SLEEP

Proverbs 3:24

24 When you lie down, you will not be afraid; When you lie down, your sleep will be sweet.

Psalm 4:8

8 In peace I will both lie down and sleep, For You alone, O LORD, make me to dwell in safety.

Psalm 3:5

5 I lay down and slept; I awoke, for the LORD sustains me.

Ecclesiastes 5:12

12 The sleep of the working man is pleasant, whether he eats little or much; but the full stomach of the rich man does not allow him to sleep.

ENJOY A LONG, SATISFIED AND PROSPEROUS LIFE

Psalm 91:14-16

14 "Because he has loved Me, therefore I will deliver him; I will set him securely on high, because he has known My name.
15 "He will call upon Me, and I will answer him; I will be with him in trouble; I will rescue him and honor him.
16 "With a long life I will satisfy him and let him see My salvation."

Proverbs 3:1-2

Section Five – The Believer's Rights & Privileges

3 My son, do not forget my teaching, But let your heart keep my commandments;
2 For length of days and years of life and peace they will add to you.

Proverbs 10:27

27 The fear of the LORD prolongs life, but the years of the wicked will be shortened.

1 Kings 3:14

14 If you walk in My ways, keeping My statutes and commandments, as your father David walked, then I will prolong your days."

Ephesians 6:2-3

2 Honor your father and mother (which is the first commandment with a promise),
3 so that it may be well with you, and that you may live long on the earth.

Isaiah 46:4

4 Even to your old age I will be the same, And even to your graying years I will bear you! I have done it, and I will carry you; and I will bear you and I will deliver you.

Deuteronomy 5:33

33 You shall walk in all the way which the LORD your God has commanded you, that you may live and that it may be well with you, and that you may prolong your days in the land which you will possess.

Job 36:11

11 "If they hear and serve Him, They will end their days in prosperity and their years in pleasures.

Section Five – The Believer's Rights & Privileges

HAVE FAITH
THE SUBSTANCE OF THINGS HOPED FOR
AND THE EVIDENCE OF THINGS NOT SEEN

Romans 10:17

17 So faith comes from hearing, and hearing by the word of Christ.

Romans 12:3

3 For through the grace given to me I say to everyone among you not to think more highly of himself than he ought to think; but to think so as to have sound judgment, as God has allotted to each a measure of faith.

1 John 5:4

4 For whatever is born of God overcomes the world; and this is the victory that has overcome the world— our faith.

Hebrews 11:1

11 Now faith is the assurance of things hoped for, the conviction of things not seen.

Section Six – The Believer & The Holy Spirit

Section Six

Having received the gift of the Holy Spirit in your heart (spirit) at the new birth, as a down payment and pledge (security deposit and guarantee) of God's intent to fulfill all His promises, you have the right and or/privilege to:

John 7:38-39

38 He who believes in Me, as the Scripture said, 'From his innermost being will flow rivers of living water.'"
39 But this He spoke of the Spirit, whom those who believed in Him were to receive; for the Spirit was not yet given, because Jesus was not yet glorified.

John 20:19-22

19 So when it was evening on that day, the first day of the week, and when the doors were shut where the disciples were, for fear of the Jews, Jesus came and stood in their midst and said to them, "Peace be with you."
20 And when He had said this, He showed them both His hands and His side. The disciples then rejoiced when they saw the LORD.
21 So Jesus said to them again, "Peace be with you; as the Father has sent Me, I also send you."
22 And when He had said this, He breathed on them and said to them, "Receive the Holy Spirit.

2 Corinthians 5:5

5 Now He who prepared us for this very purpose is God, who gave to us the Spirit as a pledge.

John 14:17

Section Six – The Believer & The Holy Spirit

17 that is the Spirit of truth, whom the world cannot receive, because it does not see Him or know Him, but you know Him because He abides with you and will be in you.

Ephesians 1:13-14

13 In Him, you also, after listening to the message of truth, the gospel of your salvation—having also believed, you were sealed in Him with the Holy Spirit of promise,
14 who is given as a pledge of our inheritance, with a view to the redemption of God's own possession, to the praise of His glory.

Ezekiel 36:26-27

26 Moreover, I will give you a new heart and put a new spirit within you; and I will remove the heart of stone from your flesh and give you a heart of flesh.
27 I will put My Spirit within you and cause you to walk in My statutes, and you will be careful to observe My ordinances.

BE BAPTIZED IN THE HOLY SPIRIT
OTHER TERMS INCLUDE: TO BE FILLED WITH THE HOLY SPIRIT, OR HAVE THE HOLY SPIRIT COME UPON YOU

Matthew 3:11

11 "As for me, I baptize you with water for repentance, but He who is coming after me is mightier than I, and I am not fit to remove His sandals; He will baptize you with the Holy Spirit and fire.

Acts 1:8

8 but you will receive power when the Holy Spirit has come upon you; and you shall be My witnesses both in

Section Six – The Believer & The Holy Spirit

Jerusalem, and in all Judea and Samaria, and even to the remotest part of the earth."

Acts 2:4

4 And they were all filled with the Holy Spirit and began to speak with other tongues, as the Spirit was giving them utterance.

Acts 8:15-17

15 who came down and prayed for them that they might receive the Holy Spirit.
16 For He had not yet fallen upon any of them; they had simply been baptized in the name of the LORD Jesus.
17 Then they began laying their hands on them, and they were receiving the Holy Spirit.

Acts 9:17

17 So Ananias departed and entered the house, and after laying his hands on him said, "Brother Saul, the LORD Jesus, who appeared to you on the road by which you were coming, has sent me so that you may regain your sight and be filled with the Holy Spirit."

Acts 10:44-47

44 While Peter was still speaking these words, the Holy Spirit fell upon all those who were listening to the message.
45 All the circumcised believers who came with Peter were amazed, because the gift of the Holy Spirit had been poured out on the Gentiles also.
46 For they were hearing them speaking with tongues and exalting God. Then Peter answered,
47 "Surely no one can refuse the water for these to be baptized who have received the Holy Spirit just as we did, can he?"

Section Six – The Believer & The Holy Spirit

Acts 11:15

15 And as I began to speak, the Holy Spirit fell upon them just as He did upon us at the beginning.

ASK FOR AND RECEIVE THE HOLY SPIRIT AS BAPTIZER

Luke 11:13

13 If you then, being evil, know how to give good gifts to your children, how much more will your heavenly Father give the Holy Spirit to those who ask Him?"

BE TAUGHT BY THE HOLY SPIRIT

John 14:26

26 But the Helper, the Holy Spirit, whom the Father will send in My name, He will teach you all things, and bring to your remembrance all that I said to you.

1 John 2:27

27 As for you, the anointing which you received from Him abides in you, and you have no need for anyone to teach you; but as His anointing teaches you about all things, and is true and is not a lie, and just as it has taught you, you abide in Him.

1 Corinthians 2:10

10 For to us God revealed them through the Spirit; for the Spirit searches all things, even the depths of God.

BE GUIDED INTO ALL THE TRUTH BY THE HOLY SPIRIT

Section Six – The Believer & The Holy Spirit

John 16:13

13 But when He, the Spirit of truth, comes, He will guide you into all the truth; for He will not speak on His own initiative, but whatever He hears, He will speak; and He will disclose to you what is to come.

KNOW THE TRUTH

Psalm 25:10

10 All the paths of the LORD are lovingkindness and truth to those who keep His covenant and His testimonies.

John 8:31-32

31 So Jesus was saying to those Jews who had believed Him, "If you continue in My word, then you are truly disciples of Mine;
32 and you will know the truth, and the truth will make you free."

John 14:6

6 Jesus said to him, "I am the way, and the truth, and the life; no one comes to the Father but through Me.

John 16:13

13 But when He, the Spirit of truth, comes, He will guide you into all the truth; for He will not speak on His own initiative, but whatever He hears, He will speak; and He will disclose to you what is to come.

Ephesians 4:21

21 if indeed you have heard Him and have been taught in Him, just as truth is in Jesus,

Section Six – The Believer & The Holy Spirit

1 Timothy 2:4

4 who desires all men to be saved and to come to the knowledge of the truth.

BE FREE

Luke 4:18

18 "The Spirit of the LORD is upon Me, because He anointed Me to preach the gospel to the poor. He has sent Me to proclaim release to the captives, And recovery of sight to the blind, To set free those who are oppressed,

John 8:36

36 So if the Son makes you free, you will be free indeed.

Acts 13:39

39 and through Him everyone who believes is freed from all things, from which you could not be freed through the Law of Moses.

Romans 8:2

2 For the law of the Spirit of life in Christ Jesus has set you free from the law of sin and of death.

Galatians 5:1

5 It was for freedom that Christ set us free; therefore keep standing firm and do not be subject again to a yoke of slavery.

Section Six – The Believer & The Holy Spirit

WALK IN SUPERNATURAL WISDOM, UNDERSTANDING AND POWER –
TO HAVE THE MIND OF CHRIST

James 1:5-6

5 But if any of you lacks wisdom, let him ask of God, who gives to all generously and without reproach, and it will be given to him.
6 But he must ask in faith without any doubting, for the one who doubts is like the surf of the sea, driven and tossed by the wind.

1 Corinthians 2:16

16 For who has known the mind of the LORD, that he will instruct Him? But we have the mind of Christ.

Psalm 111:10

10 The fear of the LORD is the beginning of wisdom; A good understanding have all those who do His commandments; His praise endures forever.

Proverbs 2:2-11

1 My son, if you will receive my words and treasure my commandments within you,
2 Make your ear attentive to wisdom, Incline your heart to understanding;
3 For if you cry for discernment, lift your voice for understanding;
4 If you seek her as silver and search for her as for hidden treasures;
5 Then you will discern the fear of the LORD And discover the knowledge of God.
6 For the LORD gives wisdom; From His mouth come knowledge and understanding.

Section Six – The Believer & The Holy Spirit

7 He stores up sound wisdom for the upright; He is a shield to those who walk in integrity,
8 Guarding the paths of justice, And He preserves the way of His godly ones.
9 Then you will discern righteousness and justice And equity and every good course.
10 For wisdom will enter your heart And knowledge will be pleasant to your soul;
11 Discretion will guard you,
Understanding will watch over you,

Proverbs 8:14

14 "Counsel is mine and sound wisdom; I am understanding, power is mine.

Acts 1:8

8 but you will receive power when the Holy Spirit has come upon you; and you shall be My witnesses both in Jerusalem, and in all Judea and Samaria, and even to the remotest part of the earth."

Proverbs 11:2

2 When pride comes, then comes dishonor, but with the humble is wisdom.

Proverbs 13:10

10 Through insolence comes nothing but strife, But wisdom is with those who receive counsel.

1 Corinthians 1:30

30 But by His doing you are in Christ Jesus, who became to us wisdom from God, and righteousness and sanctification, and redemption,

Ephesians 1:17

Section Six – The Believer & The Holy Spirit

17 that the God of our LORD Jesus Christ, the Father of glory, may give to you a spirit of wisdom and of revelation in the knowledge of Him.

Colossians 1:9

9 For this reason also, since the day we heard of it, we have not ceased to pray for you and to ask that you may be filled with the knowledge of His will in all spiritual wisdom and understanding,

James 1:5

5 But if any of you lacks wisdom, let him ask of God, who gives to all generously and without reproach, and it will be given to him.

Psalm 111:10

10 The fear of the LORD is the beginning of wisdom; a good understanding have all those who do His commandments; His praise endures forever.

Psalm 119:98

98 Your commandments make me wiser than my enemies, for they are ever mine.

KNOW THE THINGS FREELY GIVEN TO YOU BY GOD

1 Corinthians 2:12

12 Now we have received, not the spirit of the world, but the Spirit who is from God, so that we may know the things freely given to us by God,

---

BE INFORMED ABOUT AND PREPARED FOR THE FUTURE

Section Six – The Believer & The Holy Spirit

PERSONALLY AND WORLDWIDE

John 16:13

13 But when He, the Spirit of truth, comes, He will guide you into all the truth; for He will not speak on His own initiative, but whatever He hears, He will speak; and He will disclose to you what is to come.

Revelation 19:10

10 Then I fell at his feet to worship him. But he said to me, "Do not do that; I am a fellow servant of yours and your brethren who hold the testimony of Jesus; worship God. For the testimony of Jesus is the spirit of prophecy."

Isaiah 44:7-8

7 'Who is like Me? Let him proclaim and declare it; Yes, let him recount it to Me in order, From the time that I established the ancient nation. And let them declare to them the things that are coming and the events that are going to take place.
8 'Do not tremble and do not be afraid; Have I not long since announced it to you and declared it? And you are My witnesses.
Is there any God besides Me, or is there any other Rock? I know of none.'"

Isaiah 46:8-10

8 "Remember this, and be assured; Recall it to mind, you transgressors.
9 "Remember the former things for I am God, and there is no other; I am God, and there is no one like Me,
10 Declaring the end from the beginning, And from ancient times things which have not been done, Saying, 'My purpose will be established, and I will accomplish all My good pleasure."

Section Six – The Believer & The Holy Spirit

LIVE A LIFE OF POWER WITH JESUS CHRIST

John 14:12

12 Truly, truly, I say to you, he who believes in Me, the works that I do, he will do also; and greater works than these he will do; because I go to the Father.

Acts 1:8

8 but you will receive power when the Holy Spirit has come upon you; and you shall be My witnesses both in Jerusalem, and in all Judea and Samaria, and even to the remotest part of the earth."

EXERCISE AUTHORITY OVER ALL THE POWERS OF DARKNESS (EVIL)

Luke 9:1

9 And He called the twelve together, and gave them power and authority over all the demons and to heal diseases.

Luke 10:1 and 19

10 Now after this the LORD appointed seventy others, and sent them in pairs ahead of Him to every city and place where He Himself was going to come.

19 Behold, I have given you authority to tread on serpents and scorpions, and over all the power of the enemy, and nothing will injure you.

Mark 16:17-18

Section Six – The Believer & The Holy Spirit

17 These signs will accompany those who have believed: in My name they will cast out demons, they will speak with new tongues;
18 they will pick up serpents, and if they drink any deadly poison, it will not hurt them; they will lay hands on the sick, and they will recover."

Colossians 2:15

15 When He had disarmed the rulers and authorities, He made a public display of them, having triumphed over them through Him.

1 John 3:8

8 the one who practices sin is of the devil; for the devil has sinned from the beginning. The Son of God appeared for this purpose, to destroy the works of the devil.

EXPERIENCE SANCTIFICATION
SOUL CLEANSING AND RESTORATION

1 Thessalonians 5:23

23 Now may the God of peace Himself sanctify you entirely; and may your spirit and soul and body be preserved complete, without blame at the coming of our LORD Jesus Christ.

2 Timothy 2:21

21 Therefore, if anyone cleanses himself from these things, he will be a vessel for honor, sanctified, useful to the Master, prepared for every good work.

John 17:17

17 Sanctify them in the truth; Your word is truth.

Section Six – The Believer & The Holy Spirit

Acts 26:18

18 to open their eyes so that they may turn from darkness to light and from the dominion of Satan to God, that they may receive forgiveness of sins and an inheritance among those who have been sanctified by faith in Me.'

Romans 6:22

22 But now having been freed from sin and enslaved to God, you derive your benefit, resulting in sanctification, and the outcome, eternal life.

Philippians 2:12-13

12 So then, my beloved, just as you have always obeyed, not as in my presence only, but now much more in my absence, work out your salvation with fear and trembling;
13 for it is God who is at work in you, both to will and to work for His good pleasure.

BE COMFORTED BY GOD THE FATHER

2 Corinthians 1:3-4

3 Blessed be the God and Father of our LORD Jesus Christ, the Father of mercies and God of all comfort,
4 who comforts us in all our affliction so that we will be able to comfort those who are in any affliction with the comfort with which we ourselves are comforted by God.

Matthew 5:4

4 "Blessed are those who mourn, for they shall be comforted.

Psalm 147:3

Section Six – The Believer & The Holy Spirit

3 He heals the brokenhearted and binds up their wounds.

Isaiah 49:13

13 Shout for joy, O heavens! And rejoice, O earth! Break forth into joyful shouting, O mountains! For the LORD has comforted His people and will have compassion on His afflicted.

Isaiah 51:12

12 "I, even I, am He who comforts you. Who are you that you are afraid of man who dies and of the son of man who is made like grass,

AND THE HOLY SPIRIT

John 14:16 Amplified Bible

16 And I will ask the Father, and He will give you another Comforter (Counselor, Helper, Intercessor, Advocate, Strengthener, and Standby), that He may remain with you forever—

Acts 9:31 (KJV)

31 Then the churches throughout all Judea, Galilee, and Samaria had peace and were edified. And walking in the fear of the LORD and in the comfort of the Holy Spirit, they were multiplied.

BE ENABLED TO PRAY BY THE HOLY SPIRIT

Romans 8:26

Section Six – The Believer & The Holy Spirit

26 In the same way the Spirit also helps our weakness; for we do not know how to pray as we should, but the Spirit Himself intercedes for us with groanings too deep for words;

1 Corinthians 2:10

10 For to us God revealed them through the Spirit; for the Spirit searches all things, even the depths of God.

Jude 20

20 But you, beloved, building yourselves up on your most holy faith, praying in the Holy Spirit,

---

PRAY IN FOREIGN HUMAN AND HEAVENLY LANGUAGES

Mark 16:17

17 These signs will accompany those who have believed: in My name they will cast out demons, they will speak with new tongues;

Acts 10:44-47

44 While Peter was still speaking these words, the Holy Spirit fell upon all those who were listening to the message.
45 All the circumcised believers who came with Peter were amazed, because the gift of the Holy Spirit had been poured out on the Gentiles also.
46 For they were hearing them speaking with tongues and exalting God. Then Peter answered,
47 "Surely no one can refuse the water for these to be baptized who have received the Holy Spirit just as we did, can he?"

Romans 8:26-27

Section Six – The Believer & The Holy Spirit

26 In the same way the Spirit also helps our weakness; for we do not know how to pray as we should, but the Spirit Himself intercedes for us with groanings too deep for words;
27 and He who searches the hearts knows what the mind of the Spirit is, because He intercedes for the saints according to the will of God.

1 Corinthians 14:2-5

2 For one who speaks in a tongue does not speak to men but to God; for no one understands, but in his spirit he speaks mysteries.
3 But one who prophesies speaks to men for edification and exhortation and consolation.
4 One who speaks in a tongue edifies himself; but one who prophesies edifies the church.
5 Now I wish that you all spoke in tongues, but even more that you would prophesy; and greater is one who prophesies than one who speaks in tongues, unless he interprets, so that the church may receive edifying.

1 Corinthians 15-17

15 What is the outcome then? I will pray with the spirit and I will pray with the mind also; I will sing with the spirit and I will sing with the mind also.
16 Otherwise if you bless in the spirit only, how will the one who fills the place of the ungifted say the "Amen" at your giving of thanks, since he does not know what you are saying?
17 For you are giving thanks well enough, but the other person is not edified.

1 Corinthians 20-21

20 Brethren, do not be children in your thinking; yet in evil be infants, but in your thinking be mature.
21 In the Law it is written, "By men of strange tongues and by the lips of strangers I will speak to this people, and even so they will not listen to Me," says the LORD.

Section Six – The Believer & The Holy Spirit

1 Corinthians 14:14

14 For if I pray in a tongue, my spirit prays, but my mind is unfruitful.

Jude 20

20 But you, beloved, building yourselves up on your most holy faith, praying in the Holy Spirit,

Isaiah 28:9-12

9 "To whom would He teach knowledge, And to whom would He interpret the message? Those just weaned from milk? Those just taken from the breast?
10 "For He says, 'Order on order, order on order, Line on line, line on line, A little here, a little there.'"
11 Indeed, He will speak to this people through stammering lips and a foreign tongue,
12 He who said to them, "Here is rest, give rest to the weary,"
And, "Here is repose," but they would not listen.

PRAY FOR AND RECEIVE INTERPRETATION OF THESE LANGUAGES

1 Corinthians 14:13, 27

13 Therefore let one who speaks in a tongue pray that he may interpret.

27 If anyone speaks in a tongue, it should be by two or at the most three, and each in turn, and one must interpret;

BE RESTED, REFRESHED AND EDIFIED
BY SUPERNATURALLY PRAYING IN OTHER LANGUAGES

Section Six – The Believer & The Holy Spirit

1 Corinthians 14:4a

4 One who speaks in a tongue edifies himself;

Jude 1:20

20 But you, beloved, building yourselves up on your most holy faith, praying in the Holy Spirit,

Isaiah 28:11-12

11 Indeed, He will speak to this people through stammering lips and a foreign tongue,
12 He who said to them, "Here is rest, give rest to the weary," and, "Here is repose," but they would not listen.

RECEIVE REVELATION KNOWLEDGE
FROM THE HOLY SPIRIT, THROUGH THE PRACTICE OF PRAYING IN UNKNOWN LANGUAGES AND INTERPRETING WHAT YOU PRAYED

Isaiah 28:9-12

9 "To whom would He teach knowledge, And to whom would He interpret the message? Those just weaned from milk? Those just taken from the breast?
10 "For He says, 'Order on order, order on order, Line on line, line on line, A little here, a little there.'"
11 Indeed, He will speak to this people Through stammering lips and a foreign tongue,
12 He who said to them, "Here is rest, give rest to the weary," And, "Here is repose," but they would not listen.

1 Corinthians 2:10-12

10 For to us God revealed them through the Spirit; for the Spirit searches all things, even the depths of God.
11 For who among men knows the thoughts of a man except the spirit of the man which is in him? Even so

the thoughts of God no one knows except the Spirit of God.
12 Now we have received, not the spirit of the world, but the Spirit who is from God, so that we may know the things freely given to us by God,

BE MADE ADEQUATE AS SERVANTS OF GOD'S COVENANT

2 Corinthians 3:6

6 who also made us adequate as servants of a new covenant, not of the letter but of the Spirit; for the letter kills, but the Spirit gives life.

1 Corinthians 12:4-11

4 Now there are varieties of gifts, but the same Spirit.
5 And there are varieties of ministries, and the same LORD.
6 There are varieties of effects, but the same God who works all things in all persons.
7 But to each one is given the manifestation of the Spirit for the common good.
8 For to one is given the word of wisdom through the Spirit, and to another the word of knowledge according to the same Spirit;
9 to another faith by the same Spirit, and to another gifts of healing by the one Spirit,
10 and to another the effecting of miracles, and to another prophecy, and to another the distinguishing of spirits, to another various kinds of tongues, and to another the interpretation of tongues.
11 But one and the same Spirit works all these things, distributing to each one individually just as He wills.

1 Corinthians 15:10a

10 But by the grace of God I am what I am, and His grace toward me did not prove vain; but I labored even

more than all of them, yet not I, but the grace of God with me.

Hebrews 13:20-21

20 Now the God of peace, who brought up from the dead the great Shepherd of the sheep through the blood of the eternal covenant, even Jesus our LORD, 21 equip you in every good thing to do His will, working in us that which is pleasing in His sight, through Jesus Christ, to whom be the glory forever and ever. Amen.

EXPERIENCE THE MANIFESTATION OF THE HOLY SPIRIT FOR THE COMMON GOOD

1 Corinthians 12:7, 11

7 But to each one is given the manifestation of the Spirit for the common good.

1 Peter 4:10

11 But one and the same Spirit works all these things, distributing to each one individually just as He wills.

    Examples: Word of Wisdom
                    Word of Knowledge
                    Wonder Working Faith
                    Healing Gifts
                    Effecting of Miracles
                    Prophecy
                    Distinguishing of Spirits
                    Various Kinds of Tongues
                              1 Corinthians 12:8-10
                    Practical Serving
                    Teaching
                    Exhorting
                    Giving
                    Leading

Section Six – The Believer & The Holy Spirit

    Showing Mercy
        Romans 12:6-8
    (Not an exhaustive list)

OPERATE IN A GOD ORDAINED OFFICE

Ephesians 4:11-13

11 And He gave some as apostles, and some as prophets, and some as evangelists, and some as pastors and teachers,
12 for the equipping of the saints for the work of service, to the building up of the body of Christ;
13 until we all attain to the unity of the faith, and of the knowledge of the Son of God, to a mature man, to the measure of the stature which belongs to the fullness of Christ.

    Examples: Apostles
                       Prophets
                       Teachers
                       Miracle Workers
                       Healing Ministers
                       Administrators
                       Varieties of Tongues
                              1 Corinthians 12:28
                       Evangelists
                       Pastors
                              Ephesians 4:11
                       Bishops
                       Deacons
                              1 Timothy 3:2, 8-10
                       Elders
                              Titus 1:5
                              Acts 14:23
                       Preachers
                              Romans 10:14 (KJV)
                              1 Timothy 2:7 (KJV)
                              2 Timothy 1:11 (KJV)

Section Six – The Believer & The Holy Spirit

AND IN THE COMING KINGDOM OF GOD
The time of total restoration in the future

BE RAISED FROM THE DEAD
RESURRECTED

1 Corinthians 15:20-23, 26, 42, 44, 52

20 But now Christ has been raised from the dead, the first fruits of those who are asleep.
21 For since by a man came death, by a man also came the resurrection of the dead.
22 For as in Adam all die, so also in Christ all will be made alive. 23 But each in his own order: Christ the first fruits, after that those who are Christ's at His coming,

26 The last enemy that will be abolished is death.

42 So also is the resurrection of the dead. It is sown a perishable body, it is raised an imperishable body;

44 it is sown a natural body, it is raised a spiritual body. If there is a natural body, there is also a spiritual body.

52 in a moment, in the twinkling of an eye, at the last trumpet; for the trumpet will sound, and the dead will be raised imperishable, and we will be changed.

Luke 14:14

14 and you will be blessed, since they do not have the means to repay you; for you will be repaid at the resurrection of the righteous."

John 5:21

Section Six – The Believer & The Holy Spirit

21 For just as the Father raises the dead and gives them life, even so the Son also gives life to whom He wishes.

John 11:25-26

25 Jesus said to her, "I am the resurrection and the life; he who believes in Me will live even if he dies,
26 and everyone who lives and believes in Me will never die. Do you believe this?"

Romans 6:5

5 For if we have become united with Him in the likeness of His death, certainly we shall also be in the likeness of His resurrection,

---

BE FOUND LISTED IN THE BOOK OF LIFE
AND HAVE JESUS CONFESS YOUR NAME
BEFORE THE FATHER AND HIS ANGELS

Matthew 10:32

32 "Therefore everyone who confesses Me before men, I will also confess him before My Father who is in heaven.

Revelation 3:4-5

4 But you have a few people in Sardis who have not soiled their garments; and they will walk with Me in white, for they are worthy.
5 He who overcomes will thus be clothed in white garments; and I will not erase his name from the book of life, and I will confess his name before My Father and before His angels.

Revelation 21:27

27 and nothing unclean, and no one who practices abomination and lying, shall ever come into it, but only

Section Six – The Believer & The Holy Spirit

those whose names are written in the Lamb's book of life.

Luke 10:20

20 Nevertheless do not rejoice in this, that the spirits are subject to you, but rejoice that your names are recorded in heaven."

Luke 12:8

8 "And I say to you, everyone who confesses Me before men, the Son of Man will confess him also before the angels of God;

Revelation 13:8

8 All who dwell on the earth will worship him, everyone whose name has not been written from the foundation of the world in the book of life of the Lamb who has been slain.

Revelation 17:8

8 "The beast that you saw was, and is not, and is about to come up out of the abyss and go to destruction. And those who dwell on the earth, whose name has not been written in the book of life from the foundation of the world, will wonder when they see the beast, that he was and is not and will come.

Exodus 32:32

32 But now, if You will, forgive their sin—and if not, please blot me out from Your book which You have written!"

Psalm 69:28

28 May they be blotted out of the book of life And may they not be recorded with the righteous

Section Six – The Believer & The Holy Spirit

BE FREE FROM JUDGMENT AND CONDEMNATION

Romans 8:1

8 Therefore there is now no condemnation for those who are in Christ Jesus.

John 3:18

18 He who believes in Him is not judged; he who does not believe has been judged already, because he has not believed in the name of the only begotten Son of God.

John 5:24

24 "Truly, truly, I say to you, he who hears My word, and believes Him who sent Me, has eternal life, and does not come into judgment, but has passed out of death into life.

1 John 4:17

17 By this, love is perfected with us, so that we may have confidence in the day of judgment; because as He is, so also are we in this world.

ESCAPE THE SECOND DEATH
PUNISHMENT OF THOSE WHO REJECT CHRIST AS THEIR SAVIOR

Revelation 2:11

11 He who has an ear, let him hear what the Spirit says to the churches. He who overcomes will not be hurt by the second death.'

Revelation 20:6,14

Section Six – The Believer & The Holy Spirit

6 Blessed and holy is the one who has a part in the first resurrection; over these the second death has no power, but they will be priests of God and of Christ and will reign with Him for a thousand years.

Revelation 21:8

14 Then death and Hades were thrown into the lake of fire. This is the second death, the lake of fire.

ESCAPE THE LAKE OF FIRE PUNISHMENT

Revelation 20:13-15

13 And the sea gave up the dead which were in it, and death and Hades gave up the dead which were in them; and they were judged, every one of them according to their deeds.
14 Then death and Hades were thrown into the lake of fire. This is the second death, the lake of fire.
15 And if anyone's name was not found written in the book of life, he was thrown into the lake of fire.

Revelation 19:20

20 And the beast was seized, and with him the false prophet who performed the signs in his presence, by which he deceived those who had received the mark of the beast and those who worshiped his image; these two were thrown alive into the lake of fire which burns with brimstone.

Revelation 20:10

10 And the devil who deceived them was thrown into the lake of fire and brimstone, where the beast and the false prophet are also; and they will be tormented day and night forever and ever.

BE INVITED TO (AND TAKE PART IN) THE MARRIAGE SUPPER OF THE LAMB

Revelation 19:7-9

7 Let us rejoice and be glad and give the glory to Him, for the marriage of the Lamb has come and His bride has made herself ready."
8 It was given to her to clothe herself in fine linen, bright and clean; for the fine linen is the righteous acts of the saints.
9 Then he said to me, "Write, 'Blessed are those who are invited to the marriage supper of the Lamb.'" And he said to me, "These are true words of God."

RECEIVE WATER FROM JESUS
WITHOUT COST FROM THE FOUNTAIN OF THE WATER OF LIFE

Revelation 21:6

6 Then He said to me, "It is done. I am the Alpha and the Omega, the beginning and the end. I will give to the one who thirsts from the spring of the water of life without cost.

Revelation 7:17

17 for the Lamb in the center of the throne will be their shepherd, and will guide them to springs of the water of life; and God will wipe every tear from their eyes."

Isaiah 55:1

1 "Ho! Every one who thirsts, come to the waters; And you who have no money come, buy and eat. Come, buy wine and milk without money and without cost.

BE ALLOWED TO EAT
OF THE TREE OF LIFE
WHICH IS IN THE MIDST OF THE PARADISE OF GOD

Revelation 2:7

7 He who has an ear, let him hear what the Spirit says to the churches. To him who overcomes, I will grant to eat of the tree of life which is in the Paradise of God.'

Revelation 22:2

2 in the middle of its street. On either side of the river was the tree of life, bearing twelve kinds of fruit, yielding its fruit every month; and the leaves of the tree were for the healing of the nations.

RECEIVE AN IMMORTAL,
INCORRUPTIBLE BODY

1 Corinthians 15:51-55

51 Behold, I tell you a mystery; we will not all sleep, but we will all be changed,
52 in a moment, in the twinkling of an eye, at the last trumpet; for the trumpet will sound, and the dead will be raised imperishable, and we will be changed.
53 For this perishable must put on the imperishable, and this mortal must put on immortality.
54 But when this perishable will have put on the imperishable, and this mortal will have put on immortality, then will come about the saying that is written, "Death is swallowed up in victory.
55 O death, where is your victory? O death, where is your sting?"

Romans 8:23

23 And not only this, but also we ourselves, having the first fruits of the Spirit, even we ourselves groan within ourselves, waiting eagerly for our adoption as sons, the redemption of our body.

Philippians 3:21

21 who will transform the body of our humble state into conformity with the body of His glory, by the exertion of the power that He has even to subject all things to Himself.

RECEIVE THE CROWN OF LIFE

James 1:12

12 Blessed is a man who perseveres under trial; for once he has been approved, he will receive the crown of life which *the LORD* has promised to those who love Him.

1 Corinthians 9:25

25 Everyone who competes in the games exercises self-control in all things. They then *do it* to receive a perishable wreath, but we an imperishable.

LIVE FOREVER WITH JESUS THE CHRIST

1 Thessalonians 4:17

17 Then we who are alive and remain will be caught up together with them in the clouds to meet the LORD in the air, and so we shall always be with the LORD.

Luke 18:29-30

29 And He said to them, "Truly I say to you, there is no one who has left house or wife or brothers or

Section Six – The Believer & The Holy Spirit

parents or children, for the sake of the kingdom of God,
30 who will not receive many times as much at this time and in the age to come, eternal life."

John 5:24

24 "Truly, truly, I say to you, he who hears My word, and believes Him who sent Me, has eternal life, and does not come into judgment, but has passed out of death into life.

John 6:57

57 As the living Father sent Me, and I live because of the Father, so he who eats Me, he also will live because of Me.

John 14:19

19 After a little while the world will no longer see Me, but you will see Me; because I live, you will live also.

Romans 6:22-23

22 But now having been freed from sin and enslaved to God, you derive your benefit, resulting in sanctification, and the outcome, eternal life.
23 For the wages of sin is death, but the free gift of God is eternal life in Christ Jesus our LORD.

NOT HUNGER OR THIRST ANYMORE, NOR BE SMITTEN BY THE SUN OR SCORCHING HEAT

Revelation 7:16

16 They will hunger no longer, nor thirst anymore; nor will the sun beat down on them, nor any heat;

Isaiah 49:10

10 "They will not hunger or thirst, Nor will the scorching heat or sun strike them down; For He who has compassion on them will lead them And will guide them to springs of water.

Psalm 121:6

6 The sun will not smite you by day, nor the moon by night.

HAVE EVERY TEAR WIPED AWAY

Revelation 7:17

17 for the Lamb in the center of the throne will be their shepherd, and will guide them to springs of the water of life; and God will wipe every tear from their eyes."

Revelation 21:4

4 and He will wipe away every tear from their eyes; and there will no longer be any death; there will no longer be any mourning, or crying, or pain; the first things have passed away."

Isaiah 25:8

8 He will swallow up death for all time, And the LORD God will wipe tears away from all faces, And He will remove the reproach of His people from all the earth; For the LORD has spoken.

BE FREE FROM ANGUISH, GRIEF AND PAIN

Revelation 21:4

Section Six – The Believer & The Holy Spirit

4 and He will wipe away every tear from their eyes; and there will no longer be any death; there will no longer be any mourning, or crying, or pain; the first things have passed away."

BE FREE FROM ANYTHING ACCURSED
DETESTIBLE, FOUL, OFFENSIVE, IMPURE, HATEFUL, HORRIBLE, ETC.

Revelation 22:3

3 There will no longer be any curse; and the throne of God and of the Lamb will be in it, and His bond-servants will serve Him;

SIT BESIDE JESUS THE CHRIST ON HIS THRONE

Revelation 3:21-22

21 He who overcomes, I will grant to him to sit down with Me on My throne, as I also overcame and sat down with My Father on His throne.
22 He who has an ear, let him hear what the Spirit says to the churches.'"

Revelation 22:5

5 And there will no longer be any night; and they will not have need of the light of a lamp nor the light of the sun, because the LORD God will illumine them; and they will reign forever and ever.

Revelation 22:3

3 There will no longer be any curse; and the throne of God and of the Lamb will be in it, and His bond-servants will serve Him;

Section Seven

What Then Shall We Say To All This?

Romans 8:31-32 "What then shall we say to all this? If God be for us, who can be against us? Who can be our foe if God is on our side? He who did not withhold or spare His own Son but gave Him up for us all, will He not also with Him freely and graciously give us all other things?"

A brief history and introduction to the promises of God follows. As you read, you will see God enters into a legally binding agreement (called a Covenant) with Abraham, in which He promises to bless Abraham and declares that through his Seed all the nations of the earth will also be blessed.

Abraham kept his side of the agreement and by Genesis 24, we see that *Abraham was old, advanced in age; and the Lord had blessed Abraham in every way.* In Covenant with God, Abraham's wife loved him; his family was large; he walked in wisdom; and lived a long healthy life. God also made him rich. He had flocks and herds; silver and gold; hundreds of servants; along with camels and donkeys. He was known far and wide, and was respected by kings. Abraham did not lack any good thing.

More than 400 years later, God led the descendants of Abraham out of Egypt. He gave Moses the Ten Commandments, and clearly stated the blessings that would accompany a love relationship with Him, and the curses that would accompany not loving Him. Unlike Abraham, who seemed to need little instruction regarding right and wrong, the Israelites, having been enslaved for hundreds of years, were greatly in need of a clear list of do's and don'ts. God gave them the Law and the statutes; clarified the Covenant

Section Seven – What Shall We say To All This?

He was offering them and left nothing to their imagination. When they were faithful, He was faithful; when they were not, He still remained faithful. However, He was unable to bless them as He desired. For centuries they cycled in and out of faithful (and blessed) and unfaithful (and cursed).

The Covenant with Abraham, and the Covenant with Israel were steps in the process of revealing Christ. Through Whom, God established a new and better Covenant based on better promises. Under the New Covenant, the Kingdom of God is restored to the earth, and those who believe in Christ are born-again.

Through Christ, humans are offered a spiritual do-over. Those who believe in Christ are made righteous, Holy and blameless. Their spirits are restored to such purity that the Holy Spirit can once again dwell within them, without destroying them. Under the old Covenant, God could bless His Covenant partners, but could not live within them.

Ours is certainly a better Covenant. Now, instead of going to the priest for forgiveness and healing, every believer becomes a priest and a King, carrying Kingdom authority and healing to those in need. With the Spirit of Christ within us, we are now able to do the works He did and even greater works, because *as He is, so are we in this world.* John 14:12 1 John 4:17

This is an incredibly simplified presentation of Biblical history intended to awaken the hearts of those who are new to idea that God makes and keeps promises for the purpose of establishing His will on earth as it is in Heaven. Christ came that we might have life, and that more abundantly. As we appropriate the promises of God, we enjoy life more abundantly.

THESE PROMISES ARE FOR ALL WHO BELIEVE

Matthew 28:18-20

18 And Jesus came up and spoke to them, saying, "All authority has been given to Me in heaven and on earth.

Section Seven – What Shall We say To All This?

19 Go therefore and make disciples of all the nations, baptizing them in the name of the Father and the Son and the Holy Spirit,
20 teaching them to observe all that I commanded you; and lo, I am with you always, even to the end of the age."

John 17:20

20 "I do not ask on behalf of these alone, but for those also who believe in Me through their word;

Acts 2:38-39

38 Peter said to them, "Repent, and each of you be baptized in the name of Jesus Christ for the forgiveness of your sins; and you will receive the gift of the Holy Spirit.
39 For the promise is for you and your children and for all who are far off, as many as the LORD our God will call to Himself."

ALL THE PROMISES OF GOD ARE YES IN CHRIST

2 Corinthians 1:20

20 For as many as are the promises of God, in Him they are yes; therefore also through Him is our Amen to the glory of God through us.

Galatians 3:5-9

5 So then, does He who provides you with the Spirit and works miracles among you, do it by the works of the Law, or by hearing with faith?
6 Even so Abraham believed God, and it was reckoned to him as righteousness.
7 Therefore, be sure that it is those who are of faith who are sons of Abraham.

Section Seven – What Shall We say To All This?

8 The Scripture, foreseeing that God would justify the Gentiles by faith, preached the gospel beforehand to Abraham, saying, "All the nations will be blessed in you."
9 So then those who are of faith are blessed with Abraham, the believer.

Genesis 12:1-3

12 Now the LORD said to Abram, "Go forth from your country, and from your relatives and from your father's house, to the land which I will show you;
2 And I will make you a great nation, and I will bless you, and make your name great; and so you shall be a blessing;
3 And I will bless those who bless you, and the one who curses you I will curse. and in you all the families of the earth will be blessed."

Genesis 17:7

7 I will establish My covenant between Me and you and your descendants after you throughout their generations for an everlasting covenant, to be God to you and to your descendants after you.

Genesis 18:17-18

17 The LORD said, "Shall I hide from Abraham what I am about to do,
18 since Abraham will surely become a great and mighty nation, and in him all the nations of the earth will be blessed?

Genesis 22:15-18

15 Then the angel of the LORD called to Abraham a second time from heaven,
16 and said, "By Myself I have sworn, declares the LORD, because you have done this thing and have not withheld your son, your only son,

Section Seven – What Shall We say To All This?

17 indeed I will greatly bless you, and I will greatly multiply your seed as the stars of the heavens and as the sand which is on the seashore; and your seed shall possess the gate of their enemies.
18 In your seed all the nations of the earth shall be blessed, because you have obeyed My voice."

Deuteronomy 30:19-20

19 I call heaven and earth to witness against you today, that I have set before you life and death, the blessing and the curse. So choose life in order that you may live, you and your descendants,
20 by loving the Lord your God, by obeying His voice, and by holding fast to Him; for this is your life and the length of your days, that you may live in the land which the Lord swore to your fathers, to Abraham, Isaac, and Jacob, to give them."

Deuteronomy 7:11-15

11 Therefore, you shall keep the commandment and the statutes and the judgments which I am commanding you today, to do them.
12 "Then it shall come about, because you listen to these judgments and keep and do them, that the Lord your God will keep with you His covenant and His lovingkindness which He swore to your forefathers.
13 He will love you and bless you and multiply you; He will also bless the fruit of your womb and the fruit of your ground, your grain and your new wine and your oil, the increase of your herd and the young of your flock, in the land which He swore to your forefathers to give you.
14 You shall be blessed above all peoples; there will be no male or female barren among you or among your cattle.
15 The Lord will remove from you all sickness; and He will not put on you any of the harmful diseases of Egypt which you have known, but He will lay them on all who hate you.

Section Seven – What Shall We say To All This?

Deuteronomy 28:1-14

1 "Now it shall be, if you diligently obey the LORD your God, being careful to do all His commandments which I command you today, the LORD your God will set you high above all the nations of the earth.
2 All these blessings will come upon you and overtake you if you obey the LORD your God:
3 "Blessed shall you be in the city, and blessed shall you be in the country.
4 "Blessed shall be the offspring of your body and the produce of your ground and the offspring of your beasts, the increase of your herd and the young of your flock.
5 "Blessed shall be your basket and your kneading bowl.
6 "Blessed shall you be when you come in, and blessed shall you be when you go out.
7 "The LORD shall cause your enemies who rise up against you to be defeated before you; they will come out against you one way and will flee before you seven ways.
8 The LORD will command the blessing upon you in your barns and in all that you put your hand to, and He will bless you in the land which the LORD your God gives you.
9 The LORD will establish you as a holy people to Himself, as He swore to you, if you keep the commandments of the LORD your God and walk in His ways.
10 So all the peoples of the earth will see that you are called by the name of the LORD, and they will be afraid of you.
11 The LORD will make you abound in prosperity, in the offspring of your body and in the offspring of your beast and in the produce of your ground, in the land which the LORD swore to your fathers to give you.
12 The LORD will open for you His good storehouse, the heavens, to give rain to your land in its season and to bless all the work of your hand; and you shall lend to many nations, but you shall not borrow.

Section Seven – What Shall We say To All This?

13 The LORD will make you the head and not the tail, and you only will be above, and you will not be underneath, if you listen to the commandments of the LORD your God, which I charge you today, to observe them carefully,
14 and do not turn aside from any of the words which I command you today, to the right or to the left, to go after other gods to serve them.

Hebrews 7:22

22 so much the more also Jesus has become the guarantee of a better covenant.

Hebrews 8:6

6 But now He has obtained a more excellent ministry, by as much as He is also the mediator of a better covenant, which has been enacted on better promises.

Galatians 3:5-9

5 So then, does He who provides you with the Spirit and works miracles among you, do it by the works of the Law, or by hearing with faith?
6 Even so Abraham believed God, and it was reckoned to him as righteousness.
7 Therefore, be sure that it is those who are of faith who are sons of Abraham.
8 The Scripture, foreseeing that God would justify the Gentiles by faith, preached the gospel beforehand to Abraham, saying, "All the nations will be blessed in you."
9 So then those who are of faith are blessed with Abraham, the believer.

Hebrews 6:11-15

11 And we desire that each one of you show the same diligence so as to realize the full assurance of hope until the end,

Section Seven – What Shall We say To All This?

12 so that you will not be sluggish, but imitators of those who through faith and patience inherit the promises.
13 For when God made the promise to Abraham, since He could swear by no one greater, He swore by Himself,
14 saying, "I will surely bless you and I will surely multiply you."
15 And so, having patiently waited, he obtained the promise.

Hebrews 11:6, 33

6 And without faith it is impossible to please Him, for he who comes to God must believe that He is and that He is a rewarder of those who seek Him.

33 who by faith conquered kingdoms, performed acts of righteousness, obtained promises, shut the mouths of lions,

Romans 13:8, 10

8 Owe nothing to anyone except to love one another; for he who loves his neighbor has fulfilled the law.

10 Love does no wrong to a neighbor; therefore love is the fulfillment of the law.

Mark 12:28b-31

28 One of the scribes came and heard them arguing, and recognizing that He had answered them well, asked Him, "What commandment is the foremost of all?"
29 Jesus answered, "The foremost is, 'Hear, O Israel! The LORD our God is one LORD;
30 and you shall love the LORD your God with all your heart, and with all your soul, and with all your mind, and with all your strength.'

Section Seven – What Shall We say To All This?

31 The second is this, 'You shall love your neighbor as yourself.' There is no other commandment greater than these."

Galatians 5:6, 14, 18

6 For in Christ Jesus neither circumcision nor uncircumcision means anything, but faith working through love.

14 For the whole Law is fulfilled in one word, in the statement, "You shall love your neighbor as yourself."

18 But if you are led by the Spirit, you are not under the Law.

Ephesians 3:14-19

14 For this reason I bow my knees before the Father,
15 from whom every family in heaven and on earth derives its name,
16 that He would grant you, according to the riches of His glory, to be strengthened with power through His Spirit in the inner man,
17 so that Christ may dwell in your hearts through faith; and that you, being rooted and grounded in love,
18 may be able to comprehend with all the saints what is the breadth and length and height and depth,
19 and to know the love of Christ which surpasses knowledge, that you may be filled up to all the fullness of God.

Ephesians 1:18-23

18 I pray that the eyes of your heart may be enlightened, so that you will know what is the hope of His calling, what are the riches of the glory of His inheritance in the saints,

Section Seven – What Shall We say To All This?

19 and what is the surpassing greatness of His power toward us who believe. These are in accordance with the working of the strength of His might
20 which He brought about in Christ, when He raised Him from the dead and seated Him at His right hand in the heavenly places,
21 far above all rule and authority and power and dominion, and every name that is named, not only in this age but also in the one to come.
22 And He put all things in subjection under His feet, and gave Him as head over all things to the church,
23 which is His body, the fullness of Him who fills all in all.

FINAL EXHORTATION

As previously stated, 2 Corinthians 1:20 says, "For as many as are the promises of God, in Him they are yes. . ." That means that any promise you find in the Word of God belongs to you through Christ. If you find a promise from God in the Word and go to the Father and say, "May I have this promise?" His answer is already yes.

If the question is, "May I be healed?" The answer is yes. Psalm 103:3 promises, "He heals all my diseases."

If the question is, "May I be set free from loneliness," the answer is yes. Psalm 68:6NIV promises, "God sets the lonely in families."

The truth is, whatever the human need, God has a promise that covers that need. If it is common to man, it is in God's plan. Miracles should be commonplace for those who are New Creations in Christ.

The further good news is that all God's promises belong to us as a gift. We cannot earn them anymore than we can earn forgiveness of sins. It is by grace through faith that we receive forgiveness of sins and eternal life. It is also by grace through faith that we receive the promises of God. (Hebrews 11:33 . . ."who by faith . . . obtained promises . . .")

The second half of 2 Corinthians 1:20 says,

"therefore also through Him is our Amen
to the glory of God through us."

This means that not only are all of God's promises yes in Christ, but our ability to say Amen, or "*let it be so in my life*," also comes through Christ. The promises are a gift and our ability to receive them is a gift.

And finally, the Bible says that when we receive the promises of God by faith, as a gift of God's grace, God is glorified through us. That's right. When we by faith receive these gifts and are blessed, it glorifies God. If you could do it

Final Exhortation

yourself God would not be glorified. It is because it is all a gift that God gets the glory.

It seems like it should be easy to receive a gift, right? Unfortunately, receiving what already belongs to us in Christ can be hard work, not because God is withholding, but because we find it difficult to believe that He really does want to bless us. We find it hard to believe we can be healed, blessed, prospered, given wisdom etc., based solely on the finished work of Christ. It just seems too good to be true. We feel unworthy, and failing to realize that Christ made us worthy, we struggle to try to look *good enough* to God, or to *feel* like we *deserve* to ask and receive. All of this keeps us from His promises.

3 John 3:21 say's, *"If our heart does not condemn us we have confidence before God and whatever we ask we receive from Him."* Success is not in endeavoring to be perfect in our own strength, so that our heart does not condemn us. Success comes when we honor the righteousness that Christ died to give us, and boldly believe based on the fact that we are New Creations in Christ, created in righteousness and holiness of the truth. We look away from the condition of our soul and believe in ourselves as righteous spirits. We trust in God's goodness, compassion and generosity, and, led by the Holy Spirit, we connect with His power-filled grace. We believe and we receive.

We do have to put forth some effort to receive what already belongs to us. What that effort is varies from day to day. The Spirit must lead us. I encourage you to ask the Holy Spirit to teach you how to *Enjoy Your Rights & Privileges Now.* Ask Him to show you how to receive and enjoy what freely belongs to you as someone in Covenant with Christ.

To aid you in your journey into freedom, we offer the following publications.

Donna Crow Publications:
http://www.DonnaCrow.com

Enjoy Healing Now - *Jesus, EFT & Me*

By the time you finish this book, you will be fully persuaded, based on Scripture, that God wants you well.

Enjoy Healing Now will strip away all the lies that say healing does not belong to you.

But what if your heart disagrees with your head? What if, in spite of your certainty that God wants you well, you still "feel" like maybe healing belongs to other people, but not you?

Or, what if you are too sick to go to a meeting and get prayed for?

What if your church doesn't believe in healing?

What if you are so sick that you feel like you have zero emotional energy to grab hold of God's healing grace?

Well, this is where this book becomes uniquely fun. Donna experienced all of the above challenges and tells how she skillfully used a simple, self-applied acupressure technique called EFT to eliminate the emotions she had, which conflicted with her faith, enabling her to pray in faith, believe and be healed.

Her journey was not instantaneous, however, she will tell you that combining the Word of God with EFT was empowering, and made the process of getting free a pleasant one. She will also tell you she obtained what she desired, hoped for and expected—total, instantaneous healing.

In *Enjoy Healing Now,* Donna teaches you how to enjoy the process of believing for and receiving healing. If you are looking for the missing pieces to your healing puzzle, this book is for you.

> "I am slowly going through your book, and I absolutely love it! I particularly love your distinction between authority and power. It's subtle, but it is huge in its implications, and I do not think I have seen this addressed anywhere. Thank you for the fabulous work you have accomplished."
> —Sandra T

> "GOD BLESS DONNA CROW! Your book is teaching me how to pray for the first time in my life. The EFT aspect is quite interesting. Using it while declaring Scripture is awesome."
> —Kent Y

Enjoy Heaven Now

This is a book about Donna's delightful personal experience of discovering the Father's desire to lavishly fellowship with all His children.

It is intended to lead believers into a sustainable and liberating intimacy with the LORD; intimacy, which often leads to supernatural manifestations of:

Healing – Revelation – Protection – Provision – Presence

All gifts the Lord promises to those who love Him.

Does God seem far away? You can change that. Learn how to draw near to Him, so that He draws near to you. Learn how you can actually enjoy the atmosphere and provision of Heaven now, while you live on the earth, through intimacy with the God of all Creation.

> *"Wow. What a book! This has changed my life. I am doing this stuff, little by little, and being amazed. Thank you! Thank you! Thank you! I plan to share this with all my friends."*
> —Ruthanne J

Enjoy Your Rights & Privileges Now

Rights & Privileges is a compilation of the fundamental rights and privileges of the Born-again believer in Christ. It is a crash course in the abundant life Christ said He came to give us. Find out if you have been living beneath your inheritance.

"Enjoy Your Rights & Privileges Now! by Donna Crow is an exciting concise and detailed compilation of Biblical verses fielding a variety of everyday subjects of Christian and human concern. The book is a refreshing unambiguous work, shining light on Biblical interests directing the reader on the path to light regarding ageless human needs and desires."

—James Holzmann

Coming Soon:

Enjoy Extraordinary Freedom Now

EEFN asks and answers questions like:
"How free can we be?" &
"How do we get there from here?"

This is a powerful, yet fun book that challenges us all to expand our concept of personal freedom, and inspires and empowers us to reach higher than we previously thought we could.

www.DonnaCrow.com
www.fol-hs.com